Beachy ....
Angels 20

By
Paul Nash

Published by Paul Nash 2008

ISBN 978-0-9559444-0-6

Printed and bound by CPI Antony Rowe, Eastbourne

Contents

Acknowledgements

There are many people and organisations that have helped provide factual or photographic support to the work that is included in the pages that follow. I mention those that I can remember below, but at the same time both apologise to and thank anyone that I might have forgotten who has provided me with material that has helped me bring this project to conclusion.

The factual content of the book is as accurate as I have been able to make it using the sources that have been available to me. If there are any inaccuracies, I must hold my hand up to them, as well as admitting responsibility for any views expressed, whatever their relevance.

In addition to all the authors and publishers listed in the bibliography section at the end of the book, I must single out the following for their individual contributions and help. Michael Ockenden, local author and historian; Jesse Taylor, one of the local councillors in my village who was there throughout the war; the Battle of Britain Historical Society for both its efforts to ensure that we all remember what happened in the summer of 1940, as well as its wealth of factual recollections; Peter D. Evans for the detailed research on the Duxford *Messerschmitt*; Terry Gill and Stephen Wagstaff of the 249 Squadron Association, together with David Calvert, formerly of 249 ATC Squadron in Hailsham. I should finally thank my brother, Robin, for the various roles he played, from aeronautical adviser to air taxi "driver", as well as occasional artistic consultant.

Without suitable illustrations however, I fear that the prose style of the book would soon encourage the most avid reader to look for something more interesting on their bookshelves. There are many photographs reproduced here, many perhaps of less than perfect quality, but all intended to help the reader understand more clearly the way it was during the summer of 1940. I am indebted to T.R. Beckett Limited (TRB),the publishers of our local newspapers; Eddie Creek (ECC); the Chris Goss Collection (CGC); Arthur Moreton (AM) for his collection of 249 Squadron photographs; and finally Vic Mitchell of Middleton Press. Other photographs are also reproduced, but their age has inevitably made it impractical to trace their origins, and I hope anyone whose copyright may have been infringed will accept my apology, together with the knowledge that the appearance of these photographs hopefully helps younger generations to understand what happened that summer.

None of us should forget the bravery and sacrifice of all those who fought in the Battle of Britain! A few of the pilots from both sides are still here today to talk of their experiences at the time. Some I have had the privilege to meet, but they all represent the soon-to-erode tip of the iceberg in the context of the airmen that participated and, in many cases, did not survive.

Paul Nash
East Dean June 2008

Discovering
an old friend

Discovering an old friend

Cruising at 4,000 feet over the Bedfordshire and Cambridgeshire borders, the hot August sunshine flooded the cockpit. As the green fields and woods slid deceptively slowly by, Robin adjusted the radio frequency and through the headphones I heard him saying:

"Duxford approach. This is Golf Oscar Whisky Yankee November, inbound from Shoreham 3,000 feet heading 085 two POB requesting landing instructions. Over."

"Yankee November. This is Duxford. Join left-hand downwind traffic. You are number 3 to two Tiger Moths. Report on finals."

"Yankee November."

That all sounded deceptively easy. We strained to make out the runway in the slight haze ahead, to be rewarded with the sight of its lights several miles distant, slightly north of where we expected it. No sign of the Tiger Moths below, but nothing unusual about that against the background of the fields and woods.

Undeterred, we turned gently towards the airstrip. I remarked that the last time I'd visited Duxford, I hadn't noticed all the office blocks that seemed to provide a backdrop to the runway we were slowly approaching. After a brief discussion and check of the chart, we had to admit we were north of where we should have been, soon confirmed as we crossed the busy M11 motorway and spotted Duxford's hangers to the southwest.

Banking onto a westerly heading, now clearly in sight of the correct airfield to our left, we joined the circuit in time to see the last of the Tiger Moths gently touchdown. Turning onto final approach, Robin advised the tower and eased his *Nibbio* gently down onto the concrete strip.

In front of the tower stood a line of parked aircraft. Modern Cessnas, the Tiger Moths, a de Havilland Rapide, a chunky Harvard and a Stampe, were all drawn up either side of the unmistakable shape of R.J. Mitchell's iconic contribution to Britain's aeronautical heritage – the unforgettable Spitfire.

Remember the TV programme "Spitfire Pilot", where both civilian and military pilots competed for the chance to fly the Spitfire under the training conditions that trainee pilots followed during the Battle of Britain? Here was the aircraft that featured prominently in that programme, Carolyne Grace's two-seat trainer version of the Mark IX Spitfire, resplendent in its late war camouflage and garish black and white invasion stripes. A fitting start to a day that we'd planned on the spur of the moment to indulge in our mutual fascination with the war in the air during World War Two.

Today, Duxford houses the majority of the aeronautical exhibits of the Imperial War Museum, recalling its wartime role as one of the main sector airfields north of the capital. While my brother was happy to satisfy his own fascination with all areas of the flying business, both ancient and modern, I was only really interested in the contents of Hangar 4 – the Battle of Britain Exhibit.

Entering through a side door, I was immediately confronted by the bulk of an Avro Lancaster, dwarfing one of the forerunners of the helicopter, an autogyro. Between another Spitfire, a V-1 doodlebug and the fin of a wrecked *Heinkel* bomber, all in the dull camouflage colours of the time, glimpses of bright yellow paint attracted my attention.

It was an almost complete *Messerschmitt* Bf 109, looking slightly battered despite the renovation it had undergone, clearly evident from the bare aluminium panels on view. Unlike the graceful Spitfire, it retained the air of purpose and menace that everyone unfortunate enough to be on the business end of its guns must have felt during the war. The nose and rudder displayed the bright yellow tactical markings typical during the Battle of Britain to prevent the "blue on blue" problems that must have been all too easy during hectic dogfights and less than perfect visibility. These looked strangely pristine alongside some of the original scratched and faded panels. Clearly some new paintwork had been applied.

Duxford's Messerschmitt Bf 109, renovated to show it would have looked when it crash-landed near East Dean at the end of September 1940.

As I read the documents describing the exhibit, I realised with a flood of recognition that I knew something about this incident from an article many years ago in one of my brother's old Flying Review magazines. This must have been well over 45 years ago, when we both indulged in a childhood fascination with planes, aerial warfare, and Airfix modelling. I've long forgotten the details of the article published then, apart from recalling the vivid colour drawings it contained, which were useful references for modelling projects at the time.

Remarkably, this *Messerschmitt* is one of the few German fighters that have survived from the early days of World War Two, shown at Duxford close to what it might have looked like on the day it crash-landed in Sussex at the end of September 1940.

As I became engrossed in the background papers attached to the rails surrounding the exhibit, I came across a photograph, probably taken by one of the local newspaper's photographers the day after it landed, showing the aircraft under guard on the Sussex Downs. Unmistakably, in the background lies the village of East Dean where I grew up after moving from Essex in the mid 1950s.

Following a variety of family and business moves in adult life, I've now moved back to the same village and live less than 1,000 yards from where this particular aircraft landed. It became almost inevitable that I would immerse myself in unearthing the facts surrounding how this aircraft came to survive for nearly seven decades. I soon decided that I ought to examine much more closely the results of some of the other aerial confrontations during the Battle of Britain around this area of Sussex.

Discovering an old friend

I didn't then appreciate that the stretch of coastline around Beachy Head figured so prominently in the daily progress of the air war during those summer months of 1940, as well as throughout the remainder of World War Two. While not so close to the German air bases around Calais as "Hellfire Corner" off the coast of Dover, German formations frequently transited east and west along the coast off Beachy Head. They were either simply trying to lure British fighters up from their bases as part of a plan to neutralise RAF Fighter Command, or they were en route to attack targets in the Home Counties or the Portsmouth areas. German formations and lone aircraft also used this part of the coastline as one of the quicker and arguably safer routes to get back to the comparative safety of the Channel and home.

Under guard on the slopes above the village of East Dean, the Messerschmitt Bf 109 now on display at Duxford after it crash-landed in the early evening of 30 September 1940. (TRB)

Not surprising therefore that the aircraft that came down at East Dean was far from unique, with more than a dozen other aircraft, both German and British, coming to grief in the area surrounding Eastbourne during this comparatively brief but pivotal period.

In my youth the Battle of Britain remained a romantic adventure. For many like me, born in the years immediately following World War Two, this involved the adventures of make-believe heroes. Inevitably, these were themselves an amalgam of real-life characters, like Douglas Bader, Johnny Johnson and "Cats eyes" Cunningham, and the fictional airmen and soldiers that regularly triumphed in the war comics that my generation perhaps believed reflected the course of World War Two.

Today, the reality of war is much clearer, albeit second-hand, reinforced by the current cinema-vérité style of news coverage of today's conflicts, both abroad and sadly at home as well.

In my search for information and the flavour of the time, I've visited many memorials dedicated to those who fought for Britain during the summer of 1940, as well as museums run by enthusiasts dedicated to the memory of this turbulent period. None of the memorials is more graphic and powerful than the relatively new Battle of Britain memorial on Victoria Embankment, opposite the London Eye. As it should be, this is a particularly patriotic monument. It's cleverly-structured and impressive, all the more so because it was funded by private subscription, in my opinion a sad tale of misuse of public funds, like the National Lottery.

The vivid bronze panels of the Battle of Britain Memorial on the Thames Embankment portray the roles of everyone who participated, as well as the role of honour showing the names of all the pilots who took part.

We should be grateful to the Battle of Britain Historical Society for the existence of this monument, since this organisation husbanded the project to completion, collecting the necessary funds and negotiating with the various controlling government bodies. I'm also grateful to the Society for the wealth of historical information that is available on its website about the progress of the air battles over Britain in the summer of 1940. I hope everyone who visits the memorial experiences at least the emotions I did when I first saw it.

During almost four months from early July until the end of October 1940, some 537 RAF airmen lost their lives, a testament to the intensity of the struggle to defend the country from German attack. I hope the content of these pages perhaps shows a younger generation than mine the courage and sacrifice of these "Few", along with many civilian casualties, made for all of us.

It's understandably not celebrated by any of the Battle of Britain memorials, but I find it difficult, however unpatriotic, not to reflect on the scale of losses suffered by the German Air Force, the *Luftwaffe*, over this period. Contemporary records show that the *Luftwaffe* lost 2,662 personnel, an overall ratio of five to one compared to RAF Fighter Command casualties.

With most of the British casualties flying single engine fighters, almost exclusively with a crew of one, and many of the German losses being medium bombers or heavy fighters with crews of between two and five, some of this disparity is explained. However, an analysis of actual, rather than claimed, losses shows that the *Luftwaffe* lost almost three times as many aircraft as RAF Fighter Command during this violent period in our history. While some of the German airmen may well have been ardent members of the Nazi party, my impression is that many were simply professional soldiers doing what they believed was their national duty, proud of the recovery that Germany had achieved following the hardships and deprivations after World War One.

A few weeks later, during a flight with my brother in his small single engine plane on a trip from Shoreham to Belgium, I pondered on the difficulties that must have been presented by the Channel to all the wartime fliers in 1940. Robin's caution over the cross Channel passage during a calm, hot early September day gave me pause for thought. From today's perspective of the seasoned traveller, with quick and cheap travel options from the U.K. to many northern European ports and cities, we all perhaps ignore the barrier that the Channel has historically been, rather than the simple pleasure it can be today for most people.

In Hangar 4 at Duxford, Horst Perez' "White 4" is a very tangible reminder of the Luftwaffe that threatened Britain's freedom in 1940. The aircraft's starboard side is only partially-renovated, with the wing surface showing its original state on its return from North America, scratched with graffiti from that era.

How different it must have been for the German crews in the early days of the war, faced with a two-way trip from France to a hostile Britain, with the prospect of inclement weather, battle damage and low fuel reserves. Even today in a healthy, modern plane during peacetime, with the sun shining and the sea calm, the crossing from Dover to Calais was sufficient reason for my brother's caution. Imagine the potential anxieties caused by the need to nurse a faltering engine after a dogfight over the Home Counties, critically low on fuel.

The German airmen of the period coined the phrase *"Kanalkrankheit"* for the nervous feelings engendered by this. Literally translated as "Channel sickness", this conveyed the justifiable fear they all had of joining their many fallen comrades in the inhospitable English Channel. Even in summer, the water temperature rarely allowed any pilots to survive much longer than four hours without a life raft before succumbing to exhaustion and hypothermia. Of course, later in the war, Allied pilots faced almost exactly the same problems as the RAF moved more onto the offensive in the months and years that followed the Battle of Britain.

Having started this project with a very narrow geographical focus, it soon became clear that whatever happened locally is a snapshot of the experiences of many other parts of the country. While the south and southeast were the main targets of German attention, the industrial Midlands, the southwest and east coasts suffered similar attacks during the lonely months of summer 1940. This was the time when Britain became the last bastion in Western Europe against the seemingly-irresistible control of Germany and its frightening Nazi philosophy.

In 1940, faced with a passionate and persuasive Churchill, most of the British public resignedly accepted the deprivations, danger and sacrifices that Britain's isolation meant. It's difficult to see the same unified national approach today. Even the London terrorist bombings of 7th July 2005, and subsequent threats, don't seem to hold quite the same unifying persuasive capabilities as the aerial attacks of 1940 and the threat of German invasion at that time. Some of this is the result of the much wider mix of national identities that make up today's population in the U.K., with the rest of it laid at the door of the general change of attitudes over the last seven decades and the less defined nature of any threats that face us today.

So, armed with internet access and the knowledge from many years ago of a very local crash site, I decided that I should uncover a bit more substance to the circumstances surrounding this crash-landing near East Dean. In doing this, I soon found that a multitude of other people had, for one reason or another, gone before. They've uncovered a huge amount of background to that particular crash, as well as much more detail than I'd ever hoped to put together on pretty much every other aerial incident that occurred during the Battle of Britain. I am indebted to all these hardy enthusiasts for enabling me to bulk out the skeleton of my developing theme – wartime aircraft casualties around Eastbourne during the Battle of Britain.

Surrounded by the names of the pilots and the badges of the squadrons that flew in the Battle of Britain, a fighter pilot at Capel-le-Fern stares into the skies over the Channel around "Hellfire Corner".

The Battle
in context

The Battle in context

The Battle of Britain is recognised as starting on the 10th of July 1940, just over a month after the evacuation of the British Expeditionary Force (BEF) from Dunkirk. While this may seem a bit arbitrary, the reality is that it reflects the timing of the first concerted *Luftwaffe* attacks directed at Britain's economy, these being aimed at a Channel convoy codenamed *"Bread"* by the British Admiralty. The convoy became the focus of the first major air battle after Dunkirk, fought between the German units sent to attack the convoy and the British fighters dispatched to defend it. Channel convoy traffic had already been subjected to attacks by *Luftwaffe* aircraft prior to this, as had been some coastal targets around the British Isles, but these attacks had been on a much smaller scale than those seen on the 10th of July and beyond.

In British chronology, the Battle of Britain came to an end on the 31st of October 1940, some six weeks after Battle of Britain day, the 15th of September, when it finally became clear to German High Command that RAF Fighter Command remained an active and resilient force, effectively causing any invasion plans to be shelved.

While the end of October 1940 marks the end of the Battle of Britain in British eyes, this is not so readily recognised in Germany. The German air offensive against Britain continued until the end of 1940 and beyond, albeit on a smaller scale and using different tactics compared to the summer and early autumn of 1940.

Whatever the time span of the Battle of Britain, the summer of 1940 remains one of the most critical periods of World War Two, and the outcome of the aerial battles fought at that time remains pivotal to the pattern of life today. This is not only relevant to life in Britain, but in reality for the whole of Europe and the Western world. Had RAF fighter pilots and their colleagues on the ground not been able to survive to inflict the casualties that they did on the *Luftwaffe* over this period, southern Britain may well have been successfully invaded, potentially allowing Nazi domination of the British Isles.

There seems to be a reasonable case to support the belief that, while the German Army and Naval forces were actively involved in planning and preparing for an invasion of southern England, it was not necessarily top of Hitler's own agenda. The difficulties of mounting a successful cross-Channel invasion of the south coast, and the high risk of its annihilation by the overwhelmingly powerful Royal Navy, were better understood by Hitler than by many of his fawning Army and Naval commanders.

He would not have wanted to tarnish his previous record of lightning victories by rushing into a dangerous and possibly disastrous invasion of England. In reality, he was more content to allow the threat of invasion, coupled with the practical effect of the *Luftwaffe's* air offensive, to manoeuvre the British government into suing for peace. Such tactics had worked in Holland and Belgium, so why not with England?

Hitler had always seen Britain as a natural ally along with Italy in his desire to prevent communism dominating the European political map. Throughout 1939 and the summer of 1940, he remained convinced that the irresistible military forces that had brought most of Europe under his control would in turn convince the British government and its people that a peaceful pact with Germany was the most sensible outcome. In Hitler's mind, this approach also had the benefit of allowing him to concentrate on Russia, an area that became his fatal overriding preoccupation.

The importance of the Battle of Britain's outcome is all the more clear because of this. Had Germany been motivated and equipped to mount an invasion of England immediately after the fall of France, this would have led to the whole of Europe being dominated either by Nazi Germany or under the control of totalitarian Russia, neither prospect having much to recommend it. In this light, the Battle of Britain stands in history as one of the shortest and most meaningful campaigns of the twentieth century, despite its horrors and losses.

The Battle in context

With the benefit of almost seven decades of retrospective research by numerous historians and the biographies of some of the major figures of the time, it's easy to appreciate the fears, anxieties, ambitions and hopes of people on both sides of the conflict in this early part of World War Two.

Adolf Hitler had effectively conquered all of Northern Europe, from Scandinavia to the French Atlantic. Hermann Goering's *Luftwaffe* had demonstrated the superiority of its men and equipment over the air forces of all those countries, and the German Army had steamrollered over all the land forces ranged against it. The BEF had retreated ignominiously to its island sanctuary, leaving many men and most of its equipment behind in France. Confidence in ultimate victory over Britain was neither an uncommon nor a surprising attitude for most Germans at that time.

Adolf Hitler tours a conquered Paris after the fall of France in June 1940. (ECC)

After the withdrawal of the BEF from Dunkirk, completed on the 4th of June, much of both the military and civilian population of Britain would have been confused, fearful of invasion and yet typically defiant. Despite the huge losses of both men and material abandoned in France, Britain gathered its ill-equipped forces in preparation for what must have seemed to many a certain and immediate invasion. Prime Minister Winston Churchill, facing a still-divided parliament where some favoured appeasement rather than belligerence, worked hard to create for the public the myth that the withdrawal from Dunkirk was more a miracle of deliverance, rather than the defeat it effectively was. Morale was very much a strategic commodity.

Fighter Command had lost the vast majority of the aircraft sent to bolster the defence of France and the Low Countries. Some 500 aircraft were committed to the French campaign, mainly Hurricanes, complimented by Fairey Battle and Bristol Blenheim bombers, and even Gloster Gladiator bi-planes that the new monoplane fighters were gradually replacing. These heavy losses were not all the result of enemy action. Almost 50% was due to lack of spares forcing the cannibalisation and abandonment of many aircraft on the ground in the face of the rapid advance of the German forces.

Only 66 Hurricanes returned out of all of those aircraft which were eventually, and increasingly reluctantly, based in France in the spring and early summer of 1940.

Spitfires were only committed from their British bases, viewed as too valuable to risk permanently based in Europe. The relatively simple construction of the Hurricane meant that it had come into service much earlier than the Spitfire, with the result that many more Hurricanes were available at this stage of the war than Spitfires. The more challenging design of the Spitfire both delayed its entry into service with Fighter Command as well as increased the comparative unit cost to the Air Ministry.

While this left Britain with a much smaller force of fighters than Fighter Command's Commander believed necessary for its defence, by the 1st of August 1940, there were almost 560 Spitfires and Hurricanes available to defend the country against German attacks.

With the German forces seemingly content to enjoy the fruits of their victories in Europe, British industry had been granted a reprieve of almost two months before the start of the main

German aerial assault on the British mainland, allowing much of the aircraft losses from the French campaign to be replaced. Almost two thirds of this force was based at airfields in the south of the country, the area that was most vulnerable to offensive sorties from German forces now based dangerously close in France and the Low Countries

A Luftwaffe Oberleutnant examines the wreckage of a Hurricane shot down during the BEF withdrawal from Dunkirk. (ECC)

On the other side of the Channel, two German air groups (*Luftflotten*) were poised to mount offensive operations against England, the bombers on paper supported by a force of just over 1,000 fighters. These were mostly the single engine *Messerschmitt* Bf 109, but were supplemented by some 250 twin engine heavy fighters, the *Messerschmitt* Bf 110. Hermann Goering had personally favoured the development of this heavy fighter, seeing it as the way to give bomber formations fighter escorts deep into enemy territory. As the assault on Britain gathered pace over the weeks that followed, it became clear that these heavy fighters needed to enjoy the advantages of both height and speed if they were to survive against the modern British fighters.

While many British casualties during the Battle of Britain were brought down by defensive fire from the German bombers, the critical measure was parity in fighter strength. At the beginning of the conflict, the losses in France had left the RAF at some serious disadvantage in this vital area, something that British industry was able to correct during the mid-summer lull and the weeks that followed.

After the fall of France, the focus of German attention was fixed on strengthening their hold on recently-conquered northern Europe and celebrating their lightning victories. As late as the 22nd of June, when the armistice between France and Germany was signed, Adolf Hitler is said to have remarked that:

> *The British have lost the war, but they don't know it; one must give them time, and they will come round.*

Another early Hurricane, lost during the retreat to Dunkirk, is examined by Luftwaffe personnel in a French field during June 1940. (ECC)

He hoped and even expected that Britain would sue for peace, rather than be forced to devote his military resources to an invasion that would be entirely more technically-demanding than the victorious campaigns of the previous nine months. Through various neutral channels, some of his senior politicians and commanders had already been quietly in contact with members of the appeasement faction within the British government, and so it was perhaps unsurprising that he felt that patience might be rewarded by some form of peace agreement with Britain.

Recently-appointed Prime Minister Churchill was determined to oppose such moves and ultimately was successful in securing the support of his government, parliament and the people in the fight against Germany.

Hitler had already recognised that he would ultimately need to turn his forces eastwards. In the west stood Britain, still viewed by him as a natural ally, now alone and demoralised behind their formidable Channel defence, but hopefully soon to sue for peace without further conflict. To the east was Stalin's Russia, a temporary ally during the previous autumn's attack on Poland, but in the long term a nearer and more potent threat to German control of Europe, representing an aggressive seat of international communism.

German Intelligence had already detected signs of the British Government moving to ally itself with Russia in the expectation that such a move would not leave Britain so singularly exposed as it had been after the evacuation from Dunkirk.

Russia had already shown its expansionist aspirations as early as mid-June when it moved into Latvia, Lithuania and Estonia, and then expanded into eastern Rumania before the end of that month. This fear of a Russian expansion threatening his landward eastern flank and the essential Rumanian oil fields developed into Hitler's overriding preoccupation even after authorising his commanders to implement the preparations for the invasion of Britain. His fear of a communist Russia would ultimately cause his downfall.

Whatever the degree of commitment Hitler had to the invasion of Britain in the summer of 1940, it was clear that several elements would need to be in Germany's favour before any successful invasion could be attempted. First amongst these was the need for the *Luftwaffe* to achieve air supremacy over the Channel and southern England. While this was accomplished, the *Luftwaffe* would also need to retain sufficient operational strength to protect any invasion forces against attacks both from RAF forces based in more remote parts of Britain, as well as from the still powerful Royal Navy.

Second was the creation of a fleet of vessels that could transport and land all the men and material that would be required to mount an invasion, as well as maintain an adequate flow of supplies to that force as it penetrated inland. The third factor was timing, arguably the principal governing factor. This encompassed all the practical elements involved in moving a large mass of men and material across a navigationally-challenging stretch of treacherous water – the Channel – before the onset of winter.

Without demeaning the heroism and sacrifice of RAF Fighter Command during the Battle of Britain, there is a strong argument to support the belief that Hitler's distaste for naval growth, and the relative weakness that the German Navy therefore suffered from by comparison with the Royal Navy, was as powerful a factor in any lack of commitment to an invasion of Britain as were the losses ultimately suffered by the *Luftwaffe* over England in the summer of 1940.

Hermann Goering and Generaloberst von Brauchitsch waiting for Hitler's arrival for the French surrender ceremony at Compiegne on 21 June 1940. (ECC)

With a confident Goering boasting that he could destroy RAF Fighter Command given a week or two of favourable weather, Hitler was given just the reason he needed to delay authorisation of a serious invasion attempt. Goering had also presented him with a picture of the *Luftwaffe* as a much stronger and technically more advanced force than it actually was. He was always impressed by numbers of aircraft, irrespective of how effective they may have been in actual combat and how well suited to the demands of the individual theatres of operations. Goering understood this and strove to impress with numbers, seeking the favours that he knew Hitler bestowed on his successful commanders.

The *Luftwaffe* therefore found itself with most available aircraft pressed into front line service with few reserves of either machines or aircrew and many individual types unsuitable for extended action over the south of England.

A clear example of this short sightedness was the cancellation of the four engine, heavy bomber development programme in favour of the twin engine medium bombers that remained the mainstay of the *Luftwaffe's* bomber force throughout the war. The limitations of engine production simply allowed more twin engine bombers to be delivered to operational service, irrespective of the fact that the smaller aircraft carried comparatively small bomb loads and initially lacked effective bomb aiming devices.

Practical considerations of preparing an invasion fleet, as well as waiting for suitable weather and tidal conditions also mitigated in favour of delaying any invasion attempt until the end of the summer. If Goering succeeded in quickly achieving air superiority over southern Britain and London, it might have brought just the right amount of pressure on the British government to negotiate a peaceful settlement. If Goering failed, as he ultimately did, an invasion could always have been mounted at a later date. In either case, Hitler himself would have been able to shrug off any failure that might blemish his victorious record of conquests since September 1939, blaming his subordinate commanders.

It's clear from the progress of the air war over Britain during the summer of 1940 that, despite all its efforts, Goering's *Luftwaffe* in reality never came close to achieving this first goal. Even during late August/early September 1940 when British losses were causing the greatest anxiety to RAF High Command, the *Luftwaffe's* efforts fell far short of what was required.

Veteran Oberst Theo (Onkel) Oesterkamp, the commander of JG 51, the first Bf 109 unit to support the Channel convoy attacks during the initial phase of the Battle of Britain. (ECC)

Goering's hard-working air fleets were able to achieve only temporary local air superiority. The problem was that the losses they suffered in doing this would not have allowed the *Luftwaffe* to protect the invasion force either from RAF attacks from units outside the southeast, or from the Royal Navy from its various bases around Britain. Whatever the strains that combat placed on the fighter squadrons in the southeast, the other more remote air groups across Britain held a reserve of both fighter and bomber squadrons that could still provide sufficient offensive strength to cause serious damage to any invasion force in the southeast.

As a barrier to invasion from Europe in 1940, the Channel assumed unparalleled importance, as it has throughout Britain's history. It exerts enormous influence over the timing and the scale of preparations necessary for a successful landing to be made with adequate forces and supplies to finish the job. This was abundantly clear to the Allies later in the war as they made their own plans for sea-borne invasion of northern Europe. In June, or possibly at any time during the summer of 1940, Germany was ill prepared to overcome the practical problems that were unique to the Channel area.

There was no shortage of coastal and river barges that could be brought together and modified for use as German military transports for troops. In reality however, most of these were ill-suited to even a short sea crossing from Calais to Dover. They had been designed mostly for river traffic without any provision against the risk of swamping that they would have been exposed to in the swell of even a calm Channel. The transport of heavy equipment such as tanks and artillery was much more problematic, even though solutions were devised using characteristic German application and ingenuity that was commonplace in the lower ranks of the German armed forces.

Most of the barges were without their own power and would therefore need to be towed in pairs by tugs. Despite the relatively short distance from Calais to Dover, minefields, the natural hazards of the English Channel, the size of the transport fleets, their slow speed and the span of the front the German army generals planned to attack, were all major obstacles. These were further complicated by the army's insistence on attacking at dawn, accentuating the need for optimum weather and tidal conditions.

These factors effectively meant that the invasion fleet would have needed to cross the Channel during the night. Such a crossing would be able to count on little protection from the *Luftwaffe* against attack from the Royal Navy

After the German naval losses of the Norway campaign, any landing using such vulnerable vessels was under constant threat from the destroyers and capital ships of the Royal Navy, which remained a potent force.

The German naval forces were split between Cherbourg in the west, where six destroyers and various E-boats were based, and Flushing in the east, which had a complement of two destroyers supplemented by an E-boat fleet. Against this, the Royal Navy could count on two cruisers and 20 destroyers (backed up by minesweepers and motor gunboats) from bases in Plymouth and

Portsmouth, with a further two cruisers and 20 destroyers at bases in Harwich and Sheerness. This ignored Royal Navy units based outside rapid striking distance of the Channel.

An aerial reconnaissance photo of barges being massed in one of the Channel ports as the German armed forces made their preparations for the invasion of England.

Whatever defences the invasion fleet could count on from the German Navy, minefields and U-boats, the mathematics of the relative fleet strengths makes it difficult to imagine that an overwhelming number of Royal Navy destroyers could fail to destroy and swamp the major part of this unwieldy night crossing fleet.

Remarks made at the time by various high-ranking German military and diplomatic figures pointed to their lack of conviction that an invasion would go ahead at all, let alone in 1940. Some military figures admitted to adopting an approach to the preparations for an invasion of Britain that could only fall under the heading of going through the motions.

Whatever the truth of this, in the minds of the British people, as well as most of the combatants involved on both sides in the air battles to follow, the invasion of Britain by German forces was imminent in the summer of 1940.

By the 13th of July, the German Army High Command (*Oberkommando des Heeres –OKH*) presented Hitler with its draft plan for an invasion of Britain, subject to the Navy providing them with the transport they needed and dependent on the *Luftwaffe* achieving air superiority in the Channel area.

On the 16th of July, Operation *Seeloewe* (Sea Lion) was approved in principle, and Hitler issued his War Directive No. 16, calling on his commanders to make plans and conduct the preparatory steps for the invasion of Britain. The opening paragraphs of this directive translate as follows:

The Battle in context

Since Britain still shows no sign of willingness to come to an agreement in spite of her hopeless military situation, I have decided to prepare and if necessary carry out an amphibious operation against England.

The purpose of this operation will be to eliminate the English mother country as a base for continuation of the war against Germany and, if it should become necessary, to occupy the entire island.

By the end of July, once the combined planning staffs of both the German Navy and Army had made their very partisan and contradictory contributions, the target date for Sea Lion was set for mid September. This was to allow time for the required preparations, and to coincide with suitable weather and tidal conditions.

Buoyed by a confident Goering and still convinced that overtures to Britain for a peaceful surrender would ultimately be productive, Hitler was careful to forbid indiscriminate bombing of civilian targets - terror bombing - in Britain, particularly London, without his personal authorisation. As history demonstrated, this was a relatively short-lived restriction.

Relishing the glory that lay in fulfilling his claims to Hitler that the *Luftwaffe* would dominate southern Britain in a matter of days, Goering had little time for the invasion plans. He left *Luftwaffe* representation at the planning meetings to his deputy Erhard Milch, preferring to spend his time in consultation with the commanders of the *Luftflotten* that would spearhead the air assault against Britain. Despite their crucial role, there were no *Luftwaffe* representatives at the final meetings of German Armed Forces High Command (*Oberkommando der Wehrmacht – OKW*) to decide on the invasion strategy at the end of July.

Goering's men had already been testing the mettle of RAF Fighter Command in their initial

attacks on convoys in the Channel and some coastal facilities since the end of June. Their pivotal role in clearing the way for the Navy and Army to implement an invasion was passed down to them in Hitler's War Directive No. 17 on the 1st of August.

A convoy escort makes smoke as a defensive screen against Luftwaffe attacks on 14th July 1940.

The following day, Goering issued his own orders to his Air Fleet Commanders authorising the widening of the offensive operations to concentrate on military installations, particularly airfields, port facilities and aircraft manufacturing plants. This stage of the aerial offensive was given the code name *Adlerangriff* (Eagle Attack) and was to commence as soon as weather conditions allowed. *Adlertag* (Eagle Day), was the code name for the day when the first major attacks of this offensive would take place.

From the first weeks of July until the end of October 1940, the air battles that raged over southern Britain and the Channel followed identifiable patterns, as Goering and his Air Fleet commanders struggled to find a successful strategy. His earnest desire was to be able to report to

Hitler a successful conclusion of this pivotal task - destroying RAF Fighter Command as an effective force in the south of England and achieving air superiority.

The *Luftwaffe's* lack of useful and accurate intelligence on RAF strength and defensive organisation produced tactics that frequently diverted them from one potentially successful direction after another. Ironically, these changes were often made just at the point when their earlier tactics were showing signs of success, had they received accurate intelligence on their effect. Occasionally, as the offensive gathered pace towards the end of August, these had succeeded in severely damaging essential elements of the British air defence system, if only for a short period.

The *Luftwaffe* was organised into regional *Luftflotten* (Air Fleets) spanning the breadth of the countries they occupied from Scandinavia to Atlantic France. Each of these Air Fleets operated independently and in doing so limited the effect of saturation attacks on different parts of Britain's coastline that could have hindered nearby British Groups from coming to their neighbour's aid when hard pressed.

Luftflotte 2, headquartered in Brussels and with bases from Holland to Le Havre, was designated to attack southeast Britain, Fighter Command's No. 11 Group and the London area. *Luftflotte* 3, which was headquartered in Paris, was responsible for attacks on the south, the southwest and the industrial Midlands, but frequently operated in coordination with *Luftflotte* 2. In Scandinavia, *Luftflotte* 5 played only a brief but bloody role in the battle.

General der Flieger "Smiling" Albert Kesserling, the commander of Luftflotte 2, which was in the forefront of the aerial assault against the south of England and eventually London. (ECC)

Had all three German Air Fleets launched mass raids that succeeded in hitting their targets simultaneously, the outcome for Britain may well have been more disastrous. Goering's lack of talent for strategic planning did not help to resolve these difficulties for the *Luftwaffe*. Instead, it left the *Luftflotte* commanders struggling to identify individual and effective strategies that could achieve the aim of neutralising RAF Fighter Command in the south of England.

For the men of the *Luftwaffe*, already proven in earlier battles, it was a dangerous and confused period, during which many skilled and brave fliers from both sides were lost. RAF Fighter Command had to survive to fight another day, but for the *Luftwaffe*, while the overall purpose of their attacks appeared simple - destroying RAF Fighter Command - the task of achieving this aim was complex and increasingly impractical.

According to *Oberst* Theo Oesterkamp, the leader of the fighter units in the Channel area at the time, his pilots needed to achieve real fighter : fighter kill ratios of five to one. This level of success was essential if the *Luftwaffe* was to defeat Fighter Command and still retain sufficient operational strength to protect a subsequent invasion of Britain's south coast,

Initial German claims in the early days indicated that the losses suffered by the RAF would soon accomplish this task. However, German Intelligence had seriously underestimated both the front line strength of Fighter Command and the ability of the British aircraft industry to produce new machines and to repair aircraft that were simply damaged rather than destroyed. Over-claiming through the excitement and enthusiasm of intense air combat became commonplace on both sides, although subsequent examination of the reality of this shows that this was less dramatic on the German side.

A post-war analysis of the fighter losses during this period shows that Fighter Command lost 675 aircraft while the *Luftwaffe* lost 873 fighters. The inevitable conclusion of this comparison is that the *Luftwaffe* never got close to the kill ratio they needed to allow an invasion any chance of proceeding with German air superiority over the south of England.

Ironically, just over a year later and long after the conclusion of the Battle of Britain, the *Luftwaffe* finally did manage to inflict the ratio of losses on Fighter Command that "Onkel" (Uncle) Oesterkamp had hoped for during the summer of 1940. In 1941, as the RAF was conducting continuous bombing sorties on occupied Europe in an attempt to draw German forces from their assault against Russia, the roles of the *Jagdwaffe* and Fighter Command had effectively been reversed. This time, German fighter pilots achieved levels of kills that inevitably forced the RAF to curtail daylight bombing over Europe and switch to night raids, much as the *Luftwaffe* found necessary in 1940. *Plus ca change.....!*

With various *Luftwaffe* raids occurring over southern England prior to mid August, the Sussex coast seemed a likely location for a number of early casualties in the battle. However, I soon discovered that relatively few significant German attacks were made on the English mainland until the second week of August, when Goering's *Adlerangriff*, or Eagle attack, began.

The weather played an important role in this, with July showing all the characteristics of a typical English summer - rain, mist and cloud. Equally important in this was the focus of German attention on the Channel convoys, the main target until Eagle Day. Hitler had also issued a ban on over-flying the British mainland in the expectation that this would lend support to his peace overtures.

The relatively low tempo of the air war between the evacuation of Dunkirk in early June and the start of Goering's *Adlerangriff* on the 13th of August can also be linked to other factors. Both the *Luftwaffe* and the RAF had suffered heavy losses during the invasion of the Low Countries and France. The RAF had clearly lost the bulk of the aircraft committed to the defence of these countries. However, the *Luftwaffe* had also lost 36% of its own aircraft strength over May and June 1940, a fact that is perhaps concealed by the speed of German conquest in northern Europe at that time. The *Luftwaffe* certainly needed to re-equip before any serious attempts were made against England.

In Britain, increasing aircraft production under Lord Beaverbrook and a regular flow of replacement pilots from the training units and other RAF commands diluted this problem for Fighter Command. This was helped by the two month pause between the evacuation of Dunkirk and the first *Adlerangriff* sorties made by the *Luftwaffe* on the 13th of August. There was no parallel boost in aircraft production or pilot training in Germany, with the result that during any prolonged conflict, RAF strength would remain comparatively constant, whereas attrition over a long period of intensive combat would seriously weaken the *Luftwaffe*.

Germany also lacked one of the most basic goals for planning successful offensives - accurate and up-to-date intelligence on the enemy's capabilities. Throughout the Battle of Britain, German forces were unable to put together an effective intelligence network in Britain to allow them to understand the elements that became pivotal to the country's survival and its ability to resist an aerial offensive. Knowing the true strength of RAF Fighter Command and its control structure, the role of radar and the Observer Corps in providing early warning of incoming aircraft numbers, altitude, direction and strength, the tempo of aircraft production, together with the overall attitude of Britain's population, were all areas where German High Command had to rely on intelligence input of dubious quality.

The Battle in context

This failing became progressively more important as the summer passed and the *Luftwaffe* struggled, and ultimately failed, to identify effective tactics that would inhibit the ability of Britain's fighters to continue to inflict a scale of losses that the German air groups could ill afford.

Throughout the war, the basis of German Intelligence appreciation of Britain's air and armament's industry was *Studie Blau* (the Blue Report), a detailed but flawed report dated the 16th of July 1939, which confidently stated:

> ....*the Luftwaffe is in a position to go over to decisive daylight operations owing to the inadequate air defences of the island.*

The report drew the following conclusions:

> *The Luftwaffe is clearly superior to the RAF as regards strength, equipment, training, command and location of bases. In the event of an intensification of air warfare the Luftwaffe, unlike the RAF, will be in a position in every respect to achieve a* <u>*decisive*</u> *effect this year if the start of large-scale operations is set early enough to allow advantage to be taken of the months with relatively favourable weather conditions (July to the beginning of October).*

The head of *Abteilung 5*, the *Luftwaffe's* intelligence arm, was *Oberst* Josef "Beppo" Schmid, a shrewd and ambitious man who lacked two of the main qualities that might have allowed him to present a more accurate picture of Britain's readiness for an air assault - he was not a pilot and had no foreign language skills. Many of the inaccuracies in German appreciation of RAF Fighter Command's preparedness have been laid at his door. His ambitious nature often led him to highlight elements that he knew would please his boss, Hermann Goering, a tendency that ultimately prevented Goering having a realistic picture of the damage his airmen were wreaking on RAF Fighter Command and the English mainland.

At critical times over this period, the flaws in the Blue Report, meant that the Luftwaffe High Command (*Oberkommado der Luftwaffe – OKL*) persuaded itself to adopt tactics that were counter-productive to the primary aim it had. This problem was made worse by later updates that frequently added further inaccuracies.

This lack of accurate intelligence effectively gave an already muddled management faulty signals that created the wrong atmosphere of trust between Goering and his staff at *OKL* on the one hand, and the unit commanders and fliers on the other. Goering also had little talent in the management skills department. Charming though he could be, and quick to decorate his star fliers, he was always ready to shuffle the blame for the failure of his operational forays across the Channel onto the shoulders of his progressively-alienated operational subordinates.

Facing them in England was the only unified and structured air defence system in the world at the time, the principles of which form the basis of our current air defence network even today, albeit modified to deal with the demands of today's technology.

This was a far cry from the less organised reactions that the defending forces of the *Luftwaffe's* earlier opponents could muster in the face of the surprise attacks that had been a feature of German tactics since the autumn of 1939. This major difference was perhaps the most fundamental omission from "Beppo" Schmid's otherwise quite detailed analysis, a fatal one for many German airmen.

Pivotal to this was the foresight of Fighter Command's Commander-in-Chief, Air Chief Marshall Sir Hugh Dowding. It was through his determined persistence that Britain had the capability to defend its airspace.

The Battle in context

This was not just because it had the fighters and personnel to oppose attack, but because he had ensured that the fighter squadrons had the best chance of receiving accurate forewarning of potential attacks through the early warning radar stations around the coast. He had also ensured that the communications network existed to channel the required information to the most effective base for counter measures. In doing this, to some extent against the established Air Ministry inclinations at the time, he arguably laid the foundations for his later fall from grace at the beginning of the winter 1940 when the German daylight air offensive all but petered out.

Although German scientists had been almost a year ahead of their British contemporaries in radar development and the German Navy had already been using radar in naval gunnery and convoy tracking, the *Luftwaffe* had been slow in identifying the full potential it had for long-range aerial detection. In attacking Britain, the *Luftwaffe* was therefore completely unprepared for the counter measures that were in place to frustrate the sort of attacks that had proved so successful from Poland to France over the preceding nine months.

From Bentley Priory in Middlesex, Fighter Command's Headquarters, Dowding's strategic approach to managing the capabilities of Britain's fighter force was a prime factor in limiting the damage from German attacks throughout this period. He was determined that all the resources at his disposal would be optimised to ensure that his pilots were equipped to defend the country from the bombing attacks that he knew would soon come.

Air Chief Marshall Sir Hugh Dowding, the austere but effective Commander-in-Chief of RAF Fighter Command, affectionately nicknamed "Stuffy" by his subordinates.
(ECC)

Dowding had the fortunate advantage that a large part of the blueprint for this defence network against aerial attack had been planned as long ago as 1917. At that time, Major-General Ashmore was in charge of London's air defence against bombing attacks from *Zeppelin* airships and *Gotha* bombers. While he did not have the benefit of radar as Dowding did in 1940, it was Ashmore who had designed virtually all the other elements that allowed Dowding to defend the south of England. In 1917, advance warning of aerial attack would have come from a chain of huge sound locators located in the south and east of Britain, some of which can still be seen today in Kent. Radar, however, gave the whole system a new level of efficiency.

Britain's airspace was divided into four geographical or Group areas, with each Group Headquarters controlling a number of key sector stations. The Group controllers received the input of the early warning system through the filter room's analysis at Bentley Priory, allowing them to judge how best to deploy the squadrons within the Group from each sector station.

Sector airfields were the primary bases in each area, housing the sector controller, as well as several squadrons of fighters. These were supplemented by smaller airfields, as well as more rudimentary forward airstrips near the coast. In addition to being closer to respond to any incoming enemy formations, these coastal airstrips were often used simply for refuelling and rearming between sorties.

The Battle in context

The focal point of any aerial attacks from Europe was the southeast sector of No. 11 Group, with headquarters at Uxbridge. This was commanded by Air Vice-Marshall Keith Park and covered an area from west of the Solent as far north as the Suffolk/Norfolk borders. Assistance from No. 10 Group in the southwest and No. 12 Group in the Midlands was frequently called for, as the situation demanded.

The Chain Home RDF station at Bawdsey in Suffolk, showing the two sets of transmission and receiving aerials that would have been identical to the radar station on Pevensey Marshes. The Chain Home Low RDF station at Beachy Head would have been of a different design. (ECC)

Through the coordination of all of these elements, Park was able to ensure that, when a German attack was launched, a measured response was made from the available units at his disposal at the right time to counter most attacks. Through the summer of 1940, he was successful in doing this, although it was a close run thing on many occasions, particularly at the end of August and in early September.

Dowding's guiding principle was that German fighters on their own posed a limited threat, bomber formations being the main danger since they could inflict more permanent damage to his control network. With this in mind, his instructions to the sector controllers were to deploy minimal interceptors against formations that were made up of fighters alone, and to concentrate on the formations that contained a large bomber component.

Initially unaware of the capabilities of the British early warning system, German bomber pilots frequently complained that whenever they attacked in any force, there were always groups of Spitfires and Hurricanes there to counter the attack, almost irrespective of visibility. As the German claims for British fighter losses mounted, and Beppo Schmid's analysts deducted claims for British aircraft destroyed from their already-flawed information on RAF fighter strength, the cynicism of German bomber crews flying towards their targets produced the standing joke - *"Here they come again, the last 50 British fighters."*

However, when German fighter groups crossed the Channel to entice RAF fighters up from their bases, they were normally intercepted by only a token force, with the bulk of the RAF squadrons remaining on the ground.

The Battle in context

Much later in the battle, this led to some potentially dangerous errors, when the bombs being dropped on Britain during daylight had ceased to be from the normal medium bombers, instead coming from German fighters modified to carry a small bomb load. The speed and appearance of these fighter-bombers, both to radar and the observers on the ground, made them indistinguishable from normal fighters, and therefore not priority targets for interception.

When this became a more regular feature of the style of German daylight attacks in the late autumn of 1940, Fighter Command was then obliged to change its approach to these raids, fortunately by then having recovered sufficient strength to allow this. In the early days of the battle however, it was an essential tactic to avoid wasteful British losses against fighter sorties that posed only a limited threat compared to the bomber formations.

Cooperation between No. 11 Group and No. 12 Group did not always work as smoothly as it might have done. Dowding's selection of Park as the commander of the pivotal No. 11 Group area didn't please No. 12 Group's ambitious commander, Trafford Leigh-Mallory.

Air Vice Marshall Sir Keith Park, the brilliant and popular commander of No. 11 Group, who was responsible for the air defence of London and the southeast. (ECC)

Tactical disagreements on how No. 12 Group's squadrons would assist No. 11 Group when under heavy pressure from the *Luftwaffe* produced a level of cooperation that could have often been improved. Such tensions would ultimately form the basis for both Dowding's and Park's later sad fall from grace. In November 1940, after the Battle of Britain had effectively been won due in large part to the guidance and skills of Dowding and Park, both were pushed brusquely aside, victims of what appeared to be antagonism from above and also from some of their colleagues.

Even before the invasion of the Low Countries, Eastbourne and its surrounding villages had already witnessed at close hand the effect of German bombing attacks on shipping in the Channel. At 1030 on the night of Wednesday the 20th of March, the S.S. Barnhill, a 5,000 ton cargo vessel that had just crossed the Atlantic from Halifax, Nova Scotia, was attacked by a lone *Dornier* Do 17 bomber off Beachy Head.

The ship was hit a number of times and set ablaze, eventually being beached at Langney Point, where the vessel continued to burn furiously. With some of her holds flooded and others staying watertight, the vessel eventually broke up and much of the cargo of tinned food, Canadian cheeses and other material started to come ashore, much to the delight of many locals who lost little time in gathering what they could to add to their wartime rations.

Boats approaching the marina at Sovereign Harbour can still see the remains of the Barnhill even today, a potential danger for the unwary sailor. At low tide, just east of the outer harbour's entrance channel, you can see the rusting remains of the ship's boilers.

The Battle in context

For most towns along the south coast, the progress of the air war in the early summer of 1940 was measured by the tempo of German air attacks on other Channel convoys, and the actions of RAF fighters in their defence. Despite Hitler's ban on terror bombing, bombs were dropped during this early part of the summer over coastal towns in the south of England, as well as other parts of the country.

With her back broken, the S.S. Barnhill lies off Langney Point, close to the entrance channel of today's Sovereign Harbour marina. (TRB)

Eastbourne recorded its first bombing just before midday on the 7th of July, when a stick of bombs was dropped by a lone bomber over the St. Phillips Avenue area, killing one and wounding several others. Similarly, Hastings suffered its first bombing attack early on the 26th of July, when another lone bomber dropped 11 bombs over the West Hill and the Cricket Ground areas. Most coastal towns in southern England suffered in this way, but the main bombing of these areas was really not to start in earnest until September and beyond. Some of these attacks may have been stimulated by the military takeover of coastal hotels and private schools, and it would be charitable to assume that others may have been the result of navigation errors in bad weather.

The Channel - Kanalkampf:
10th July - 11th August

The Channel - Kanalkampf : 10th July-11th August

While German control of occupied Europe was being celebrated and consolidated, no real cohesive strategy was developed for offensive sorties against Britain. Hitler remained convinced that a peaceful settlement with Britain was a natural progression of the victories in Europe and was content to allow the *Luftwaffe* to encourage this by neutralising RAF Fighter Command in southern Britain. Goering and his *Luftflotte* commanders formulated their own tactics without of any overall guiding strategy from their Commander-in-Chief.

In the *Luftwaffe* operational orders for the 2nd of July 1940, two objectives were identified - closing the Channel to English shipping and clearing the area of British fighters. From their new bases in the Low Countries and northern France, the *Luftwaffe* units began attacks on the convoys around Britain's coast, particularly in the Channel.

These initial sorties were fundamentally probing moves, aimed at evaluating RAF Fighter Command's strength and reaction times, as well as destroying any British fighters that rose to intercept. The secondary aim was damaging Britain's import infrastructure, heavily dependent for food and war material on shipping from overseas. There were various bombing sorties against major port facilities in Portsmouth, Falmouth, Swansea, Newcastle and Merseyside, but it was the shipping strikes against convoys in the English Channel that dominated the early weeks of the campaign.

Goering dedicated two veteran commanders in *Luftflotte 2* to the task of closing the Channel to British shipping and testing RAF strength and response times. *Oberst* (Group Captain) Johannes Fink, *Geschwaderkommodore* of the bomber unit KG (*Kampfgeschwader)* 2, was made *Kanalkampffuehrer* (Head of Channel Operations), despite his comparatively advanced age of 50. His bomber group was supported by two *Gruppen* (Wings) of *Junkers* Ju 87 *Stuka* dive-bombers and the fighter unit *Jagdgeschwader* (JG) 51, flying *Messerschmitt* Bf 109s. The heavy fighter group, *Zerstoerergeschwader* (ZG) 26 was also incorporated into *Luftflotte 2*, although this was based further inland around Lille and St. Omer, since the Bf 110 had greater fuel range.

The fighter component of this force was led by *Oberst* Theo Oesterkamp, a veteran of World War One who had been responsible for 32 allied aircraft destroyed in that earlier conflict. It was Oesterkamp who developed the theory that his *Jagdwaffe* units would need to inflict losses of at least five to one in Germany's favour against the RAF if they were to meet the criteria to allow an invasion to be mounted with any chance of success. During some of the early days of the fighting, the *Luftwaffe* kill ratio indeed exceded Oesterkamp's magic 5:1 ratio, on some days by some considerable margin. These early successes served to reinforce German views that RAF Fighter Command was rapidly deteriorating and would soon become a depleted force.

Together, the two older leaders conducted a campaign with some considerable skill, allowing them to locate the convoys, sink some of the ships, as well as evaluating the response from British fighters to the offensive threats of this new stage of the war. On the 27th of July, "*Onkel*" Theo Oesterkamp was made *Jagdfliegerfuehrer* 2, in charge of all fighter operations for the whole of *Luftflotte 2*, and his position as leader of JG 2 was taken over by the brilliant Werner Moelders, one of Germany's younger rising aces.

The fighter strength of *Luftflotte 2* was expanded in the Pas de Calais area in order to minimise the effect of the limited range of the *Messerschmitt* Bf 109, the only interceptor then in the *Luftwaffe's* arsenal that could compete with the RAF's Hurricanes and Spitfires. JG 51 was joined by JG 3, JG 26, JG 52 and JG 54, most squadrons being based at improvised airstrips on farmland in a radius around Calais. Many of these Channel operations were additionally supported by sorties from *Luftflotte 3* fighter units, operating from bases further west in France.

The fuel limitations of the Bf 109 remained a problem for the *Luftwaffe* throughout the Battle of Britain. It's readily acknowledged that, had external fuel tanks been fitted to the aircraft early on in the war, many German casualties, either unescorted bombers or fighters ditching in the Channel out of fuel, would probably not have occurred.

Generalmajor Wolfram von Richthofen (left), cousin to the Red Baron of World War One fame, was the commander of the Stuka units of Fliegerkorps VIII, part of Luftflotte 3. Here he enjoys a joke with Albert Kesserling , the commander of Luftflotte 2. (ECC)

It's still debated by some whether such a technical modification would have had a radical effect on the strategic balance, but limited fuel range for both German and British single engine fighters remained a tactical limitation that undoubtedly caused casualties. Fortunately for Britain, while some fuel tanks were available for use by the *Luftwaffe*, their wooden construction caused them to be considered unsafe to use due to the risk of leaks, so they were generally not employed until later in the war.

For Dowding, with his fighter force already seriously depleted by a larger commitment than he had wanted in support of France and the BEF over the preceding months, the convoy attacks presented him with an extra problem. His concern was to preserve as much of Fighter Command as possible to provide southern England with a cohesive air defence against the bombing attacks that he knew would come. He knew how exposed his fighter pilots would be over the Channel.

The fighter losses suffered over the early part of the summer in a vain attempt to stem the rapid German conquest of northern Europe made it all the more essential to conserve remaining RAF fighter strength. Almost 90% of the aircraft sent to the Low Countries and France had been lost there.

While he strove to retain as many fighters as he could for the eventual bomber onslaught, he was unable to ignore the convoys' protection and was forced to allocate what he saw as wasteful standing patrols over the convoys that transited the Channel during daylight. Until the vulnerability of daylight convoys passing through the Straits of Dover was demonstrated by the scale of shipping losses, RAF pilots operating over the Channel were at risk, not just from the *Luftwaffe*, but also from the inhospitable waters of the Channel.

Following the last major convoy on the 8th of August, daylight convoys through the Dover Straits were stopped and the standing convoy patrols became thankfully redundant. With their disappearance, Dowding was relieved of the fear for his pilots' exposure operating over the Channel, with its accompanying risk of baling out over the sea.

When they were necessary, these standing patrols were normally made up of sections of three aircraft, or sometimes a whole flight of six, operating over whatever convoy traffic may have been passing through their area of responsibility. When the ships were attacked by a squadron of *Stukas* or other German bombers, these would normally be escorted by at least a *Gruppe* of fighters (usually 40 – 45 aircraft), some close by but mostly high overhead.

Since this was happening often in full view of the coastal population, it's easy to see how the concept of "The Few" RAF fighters was fostered. The imbalance in numerical strength was highly visible and there was little time to reinforce the standing patrol before the bombers had dropped their bombs and returned to France. Even when the standing patrols themselves had additional aircraft covering their progress from a high vantage point, there was seldom parity of fighter strength between the two adversaries.

An additional danger at this stage of the war was that there was no formal air-sea rescue service available for ditched RAF pilots. Very few, unfortunate enough to be forced to abandon their aircraft over the Channel, were recovered alive during the Battle of Britain. Careful to conserve his pilots and aircraft for the coming German onslaught, Dowding was anxious to limit his pilots' exposure over the Channel for this reason as much as any other.

British fighter pilots were equipped simply with Mae-West inflatable flotation vests and the hope that, if they baled out over the sea, they would be spotted and picked up, either by nearby fishing boats, the Royal Navy or the lifeboat service. This shortcoming was to be corrected over time, but too late to have any positive effect on pilot recovery during this period of the war, when the defence of the convoys inevitably meant a high risk of casualties in the sea.

A convoy passing through the Channel during early August 1940 comes under attack from Luftwaffe bombers. Exploding flak dots the sky around the German aircraft andthe exploding bombs raise fountains of water around the vessels.

The *Luftwaffe* was meanwhile addressing this issue with a variety of alternatives. Roving E-boats supplemented a chain of floating rescue buoys, while float-planes adapted for the task of aircrew recovery were on call. Many *Luftwaffe* aircraft were supplied with inflatable rafts and pilots were equipped with marker dye packs to identify their position in case of ditching in the sea. Even so, it's probable that the majority of the *Luftwaffe* pilots listed as "missing" in the casualty returns fell victim to the cold neutrality of the Channel, whether the result of combat damage, running low on fuel, or both.

For the *Luftwaffe*, it nevertheless appeared to be a win, win situation. If the British fighters didn't come to defend the convoys, the ships would be sunk or damaged, and if the fighters did come to the convoys' defence, both sides would inevitably suffer losses. The Germans felt they could withstand this for the limited time they expected before RAF Fighter Command was a spent force. Initial German intelligence on Britain's fighter defence force and its reserves pointed to the RAF soon running out of both men and machines.

Later analysis showed that the reverse of this was actually true, since Britain had refined the process of replacing both machines and pilots, however tight pilot availability was later in the battle. Fundamentally, the Germans lacked both those reserve capabilities in a prolonged war of attrition. Hermann Goering and his *Luftwaffe* anticipated a repeat of the quick and easy victories it had achieved in Poland, Holland, Belgium and France. None of them expected to be thrown into the meat grinder that the battle over southern England became over the long summer of 1940.

On 9 July 1940, this Heinkel He 59 float-plane was forced down over the Goodwin Sands and later towed to Deal by the Walmer lifeboat. There was much controversy over what the Germans viewed as part of the Red Cross being attacked by British fighters. Dowding saw them as fair game since they rescued downed German aircrew who could fight another day.

Local Casualties 10th July – 11th August 1940

1.   Spitfire of 64 Squadron on 17th of July crash-landed in Hailsham

Typical of the weather in the southeast at the time, the 17th of July was dull and overcast with occasional rain throughout the country. For the experienced hunter in the air, the cloud cover provided concealment both for stalking unwary victims and subsequent escape, a near-perfect scenario for the battle-experienced pilots of the *Jagdwaffe* and their high-flying Bf 109s.

Flying Officer Donald Taylor of 64 Squadron was on patrol over the Channel with the 13 Spitfires of his squadron colleagues. He had the misfortune to be operating behind the remainder of the squadron as the "weaver", whose purpose was to prevent his colleagues from being attacked from behind. Sadly, there was nobody to provide the same protection for him, typical of this precarious role, and he was "bounced" off Beachy Head.

Leutnant (Pilot Officer) Helmut Wick of 3rd *Staffel*/JG 2 (Richthofen) made a diving attack on Taylor and then disappeared back into the cloud cover before the remaining British pilots had a chance to react.

Lt. Wick and his wingman, *Lt.* Franz Fiby had been dispatched from their base in Northern France to intercept a Blenheim bomber returning to England after a mission over France. The two German fighters failed to find the bomber, but eventually saw through the cloud cover that they had ventured over the English coast. Despite their standing orders at this time forbidding them from venturing over England, *Lt.* Wick was hungry for some target to attack, so he decided to stay a little longer over the area to see if any targets presented themselves. Conveniently, 14 Spitfires from 64 Squadron soon appeared below the broken cloud cover.

Wounded in the attack and fighting for control over the coast, Donald Taylor managed to force-land his seriously-damaged Spitfire (P9507) at 1400 hours near Hempstead Lane in Hailsham, from where he was sent to hospital in Eastbourne. Like many British fighters that managed to land with varying degrees of battle damage, his Spitfire was later recovered for repair, contributing to German over-estimation of the success of their efforts to destroy RAF Fighter Command.

Here three flights of Spitfires show how much attention had to be focused on position in the formation, rather than quartering the sky for lurking German fighters.

At this early stage of the battle, the experience that the German fighter groups had gained from their earlier combat missions, and the flexibility of the formations they adopted, allowed them to take advantage of the more cumbersome practices and inexperience of many RAF pilots. With the excellent high altitude performance of the Bf 109, German fighter units generally operated *freie Jagd* (literally free hunting) offensive sweeps at 25,000 feet or more, giving them the ability to spot enemy formations below and manoeuvre into the classic position to attack unobserved out of the sun.

Frequently, when the German aircraft had not been spotted by their intended prey, the leader would dive alone to attack the rearmost British aircraft and then use the airspeed gained in the dive to zoom back up to the German formation. It was not unknown for several such diving attacks to be made before the remainder of the British formation became aware they were under attack, having already lost some of their colleagues while they were concentrating on their regulation formations.

This particular episode, and many like it, clearly showed how much the German fighter pilots had learned during their earlier battles in Spain and northern Europe. Surprise, speed and accuracy of attack again proved as important in 1940 as they had been over the Western Front 23 years earlier.

Typically, German fighter formations operated in pairs, one pair forming a *"rotte"*, each pair made up of a leader, who would perform the attack, and a wingman who would protect the leader from behind and usually slightly below. A *rotte* would combine with another to become a *"schwarm"* (four aircraft) of two *"rotten"*, three *"schwarmen"* would make up a *"Staffel"* (twelve aircraft), and four *"Staffeln"* (Including a *"Stab"* or Headquarter's *Staffel*) would make up a *"Gruppe"* which could contain some 40-45 aircraft. Three *"Gruppen"* would make up a *"Geschwader"*, at full strength almost 150 aircraft.

Normally, the first three *Staffeln* would make up the complement of I.*Gruppe*, with II.*Gruppe* comprising the next three. Thus *Lt.* Wick and *Lt.* Fiby, flying with the 3rd *Staffel*, were part of I.*Gruppe*/JG 2. Each of the *Staffeln* in the *Gruppe* would carry colour coded identifying numerals or letters, usually green for the *Stab Staffel*, with the other nine *Staffeln* being coded white, red (sometimes black) or yellow (sometimes brown) in sequence. In this way the 2nd *Staffel* (I.*Gruppe*) would have individual aircraft identification numbers shown on the fuselage in red (or black), while the 3rd *Staffel* (I.*Gruppe*) would have yellow numbers. At the time, Wick's normal aircraft was "Yellow 2". Other identifying marks aft of the fuselage national insignia showing the *Gruppe* symbol followed similar colour patterns.

A schwarm of Messerschmitt Bf 109s from the 4th Staffel JG 26, showing the typical finger-four formation that the German crews had adopted since their operational experiences during the Spanish Civil War. Here the formation is slightly closed up for the benefit of the camera.

Each *schwarm* would operate in a loose finger-four formation, where the aircraft were positioned similar to the outstretched fingers of one hand. This allowed each of the pilots to watch the blind spots of their companions and, being positioned some distance apart, the pilots of the *schwarm* could concentrate on spotting enemy aircraft rather than maintaining close formations. This structure was so suited to the tactics required for fighter operations that it remains the standard format for most fighter units throughout the world even today.

By comparison, British fighter units then operated in sections of three aircraft close together, either in a V-formation or in line astern, following RAF regulation training. These demanded from the pilots a degree of concentration on aircraft positioning within the flight that could more effectively have been used looking out for the enemy, especially behind and above. The insistence on tight formations meant that it was generally only the flight leader who would be on the look-out for enemy aircraft, the other two flight members being forced to devote most of their attention to maintaining position in the formation.

Sections of three aircraft, each identified by different colours (red, yellow, blue or green), were arranged with two sections forming a flight ("A" or "B") and two flights per squadron. Individual aircraft would be identified by their section colour and by a number in each section, such as Red One (Red flight leader), Red Two and Red Three. Squadron strength was typically 12-15 serviceable aircraft, with some pilots and aircraft in reserve. Squadron formations often used one or two "weaver" aircraft operating behind the main group, whose purpose was to protect from unseen attack from behind.

Before the collapse of the Low Countries and France, British fighter formations had been developed with the sole aim of dealing with unescorted bombers attacking Britain from bases in Germany. Since the Bf 109 did not have the fuel duration to escort bombers to Britain from Germany, this was perhaps a justifiable strategy.

Training and tactics for British fighter pilots at the time centred on precise formation attacks that were viewed as the logical approach to bringing down unescorted bombers. On reaching the point of interception, the leader of each RAF formation would decide which of six set-piece attack formations to use, depending on the direction the attack was to be made from – astern, beam, above or below – and how many aircraft were involved.

These Fighting Area Attacks (FAA), as they were called, were developed in the inter-war years to take account of the huge technological developments in aircraft design, power and armament that had been seen during the 1930s. They were the cornerstone of the final training for British fighter pilots, and the basis of most fighter units' operations during the early stages of the war.

With the high performance of the new monoplane fighters operated by both British and German front-line units, the Air Ministry's philosophy was that the sort of dog fighting that had been experienced in the First World War would be impractical because of the much greater stresses on both pilots and aircraft that the higher levels of performance meant. The Air Ministry saw the fighters' role as attacking incoming unescorted bomber formations, a task for which the Fighting Area Attacks were designed. In practical terms, they presented a very pretty spectacle at peacetime air displays but they were fatally unsuited to the demands of the hectic air battles over southern England during the summer of 1940.

With German fighter units occupying bases in the Pas de Calais after the fall of France, these theories rapidly became redundant. Few German bomber formations ventured knowingly over Britain in daylight without swarms of Bf 109 and Bf 110 fighters in attendance. In most cases, the escorting fighters were frequently out of sight behind sun and cloud, 10 - 15,000 feet above the bombers.

With the intercepting British formations frequently clawing for some height advantage to attack the bombers at their normal height of between 15,000 and 18,000 feet, the German fighter units were often noticed only when losses at the rear of the British formations were already being suffered. Even the standing patrols over the Channel convoys were rarely much above 15,000 - 18,000 feet, and frequently they were much lower.

The vulnerability of these British tactics inevitably put pressure on the pilots themselves to evolve formations that were more survivable. As the Battle for France came to an end and the Battle of Britain followed, they began to adopt patterns that were more akin to the German methods.

This happened neither officially nor quickly enough to prevent many casualties such as Donald Taylor, victims as much of RAF regulations and inflexible training methods as the stalking skills of the German fighter units. In this early part of the conflict, the exceptions to this rule tended to be the squadrons that had already been blooded during the first half of 1940 over Europe. Most of these had soon adapted to formation tactics that were much more in line with those of their *Luftwaffe* adversaries.

Throughout the Battle of Britain, as circumstances demanded, Dowding rotated tired but battle experienced squadrons to quieter areas outside No. 11 Group, replacing them with fresh squadrons from these quieter parts of the country. These were mostly new to combat and, while they may have been made up of experienced fliers, they would mostly employ the formation attack manoeuvres that RAF regulations required them to do. For the growing list of German fighter *experten* (aces) cruising at high altitude over the Channel and southern Britain, the appearance of a British squadron in tight formation below was an open invitation for a bounce attack. Not for nothing did the *Luftwaffe* pilots call the RAF formations *idiotenreihen* or "rows of idiots".

Lt. Wick was rapidly honing the skills of the hunter/killer required of all successful fighter

pilots during the Battle of Britain. With his unit operating within *Luftflotte 3* from bases around Le Havre, he was already an *expert*, having established a reputation as an aggressive and skilled fighter pilot, with a tally of 13 kills, mostly in the invasion of the Low Countries and France. Donald Taylor's aircraft became his 14th kill and the first Spitfire that he had so far shot down. It was not to be his last. In the period up until the end of October 1940, Helmut Wick had achieved a tally of kills totalling 44 aircraft, including a further 16 Spitfires and 13 Hurricanes.

Helmut Wick with Adolf Hitler on 6 October 1940 at the Berchtesgarten on the occasion of his award of the Knight's Cross with Oak Leaves. (ECC)

He became *Staffelkapitan* (roughly equivalent to a British Squadron Leader) of 3rd *Staffel*/JG 2 on the 1st of August, having effectively led this unit since the 23rd of June. On the 7th of September, he achieved the rank of *Gruppenkommandeur* (roughly equivalent to a British Wing Commander) of I.*Gruppe*/JG 2. He was awarded the Knight's Cross with Oak Leaves on the 6th of October, by no less than Adolf Hitler himself. Helmut Wick became the youngest *Major* in the *Wehrmacht* and was appointed *Kommodore* (roughly equivalent to a British Group Captain) of JG 2 by Hermann Goering on the 20th of October.

He had achieved a list of aircraft kills that put him neck and neck with other well-known German aces of the time, such as Adolf Galland and Werner Moelders. Inevitably, his successes made him a natural target for the German propaganda machine and, like Galland and Moelders, his photograph was frequently in the German press as his list of aerial victories grew.

Finally, late in the afternoon of the 28th of November, after achieving 56 victories and briefly becoming the joint top *Jagdwaffe* scorer with Adolf Galland, Wick was himself shot down near the Isle of Wight by Flight Lieutenant John Dundas of 609 Squadron, never to be seen again.

Oberleutnant Rudi Pflanz had been flying as part of the *Stabschwarm* (four aircraft from the Headquarters Flight) of JG 2 with Franz Fiby, his own wingman. He reported seeing Wick's aircraft being shot down by John Dundas, with Wick baling out into the sea 50 kilometres southwest of the

Isle of Wight. The unit records show him simply as one of the many who were "missing". Rudi Pflanz quickly made recompense for the loss of JG 2's *Kommodore*.

> *After I had lost Fiby, I went low and turned for home. I saw two aircraft in front of me which I flew towards. Too late I recognised the second as a Spitfire. It shot down the Messerschmitt Bf 109 and the pilot baled out. I then shot the Spitfire down; the pilot came down in the sea, I then began talking to the rescue services.*

Ironically, Helmut Wick had taken off just before the arrival of orders taking him off offensive operations since he had become too valuable to risk losing in action. Driven by the race to establish his position as the highest scoring German fighter ace, Helmut Wick became as much the victim of German propaganda as he was of John Dundas, who was also posted as missing after this action.

Helmut Wick's Messerschmitt Bf 109 E prior to take-off from Beaumont-le-Roger in France.

The South Coast - Adlertag:
12th - 23rd August

The South Coast - Adlertag : 12th - 23rd August

With the *Luftwaffe's* long-range flights over the Atlantic forecasting improved weather conditions for the Channel and southern England, Eagle Day was finally scheduled for the 13th of August. This was the signal to switch from the probing strategy against the Channel convoys of the previous few weeks. From this point, it was to be an all-out air offensive against RAF fighter bases and their support infrastructure, port facilities, coastal radar installations and aircraft production plants throughout the country.

The plan was to start attacking the targets near the south coast and then to gradually work towards those that were closest to London. The expectation was that by the time the coastal facilities had been taken out of operation and targets near London were being decimated, Fighter Command would be sufficiently damaged to minimise the threat it posed, and the British Government would sue for peace. Ideally, the former would stimulate the latter.

Goering and his commanders soon made one of the most flawed tactical decisions of the campaign. After early raids on the curious masts of the south coast's radar installations which had no apparent effect, sorties against radar installations were dismissed by Goering as virtually irrelevant, and the full weight of the *Luftwaffe* attacks was directed against more tangible targets – the airfields. While he was happy to encourage the development of ever faster and better armed aircraft, Goering distrusted new technology that he didn't understand and offered less obvious benefits. Ignoring radar became one of his biggest mistakes.

In taking the decision to leave the radar stations largely unmolested, he and his staff demonstrated their real lack of understanding of the important role played by Britain's radar facilities within the country's early warning network. Without radar, the only early indication of the build up of an impending raid was normally from the long range radio listening posts identifying how many aircraft were being prepared for take-off as each German aircraft tested its radio prior to departure. Without radar, until the Observer Corps was physically able to see the attacking formations as they approached and crossed the coast, there was limited scope to define the types of aircraft approaching, the scale of each formation, as well as its height and direction. With poor visibility, low cloud, rain and mist, typical in southern England even during the summer, the Observer Corps defaulted to audible detection methods with all their limitations. Had Goering persevered with continuous attacks on the radar facilities, the outcome of the battle would probably have been altogether different.

For many of the targets attacked by the *Luftwaffe*, either the inbound flight, or the eventual escape back to northern French bases, involved a route along the Sussex coastline or over the South Downs. Frequently over this period, "Smiling Albert" Kesserling, the commander of *Luftflotte* 2, would continue to send formations of fighters along the Channel coast in the hope that it would tempt British fighter squadrons into the air to suffer losses by attrition, thus reducing the RAF's ability to intercept later bomber formations. Sometimes, the instructions to the Group controllers to wait for the bombers were either ignored, or the recall instruction to scrambled squadrons received too late to prevent British casualties.

If you appreciate the scale of the offensives that the *Luftwaffe* organised in the days immediately following Eagle Day, it's easy to understand why the middle of August figures so prominently in the list of aircraft brought down in the Eastbourne area. On the 13th of August alone, something approaching 600 German aircraft attacked targets over southern England throughout the day. While these sorties damaged a number of airfields like Eastchurch, Detling, Odiham and Farnborough, these were not the Fighter Command sector airfields that the *Luftwaffe* should have been so intent on destroying, further underlining the *Luftwaffe's* lack of meaningful basic intelligence on the workings of RAF Fighter Command.

Few of the airfields bombed had any relevance to the all-important target - Fighter Command, its aircraft, pilots and communications network. Detling was a Coastal Command base, Farnborough the home of the Royal Aircraft Establishment, largely involved in aircraft testing and evaluation. Eastchurch was another Coastal Command base, although 266 Squadron's Spitfires had been using it occasionally alongside Coastal Command's Blenheims.

His expression for once belying his nickname, Albert Kesserling discusses the early days of the air offensive against Britain with some of his Luftflotte 2 staff on the cliffs overlooking the Dover Straits. (ECC)

The *Luftwaffe* regularly dispatched high-flying reconnaissance aircraft over Britain, with the aim of identifying the current level of activity at the targets scheduled for the day's sorties, as well as clarifying the effect of earlier raids. Despite the slim chance of British fighters actually gaining enough height to be able to intercept these high-flying and largely lightly armed intruders, Fighter Command regularly scrambled sections of fighters in an effort to do exactly that. Rarely successful given the height advantage of the incoming reconnaissance aircraft, the benefit of this was that the German intruders were forced to stay at heights that prevented their photographs from being detailed enough in certain critical areas.

Despite the best of German camera technology, from the height at which the reconnaissance aircraft were forced to fly, it was difficult to define accurately aircraft types on the ground. The difference in profile between single and multi engine aircraft was clear enough, but identifying types of single engine aircraft was more prone to error. Not all airfields with single engine aircraft on the ground, particularly around the coast where the German offensive started, were fighter bases, apart from the sector station at Tangmere.

As August passed and the German offensive moved its focus from the coast inexorably towards London, it became clear that it was the Fighter Command sector stations around London that were the important targets. As the bombing raids focussed increasingly on the London outskirts, late August was to see more attention paid to Biggin Hill, Kenley, Hornchurch, as well as to Tangmere.

The 15th of August saw some 2,000 German aircraft involved in sorties that were predominantly directed against these sector airfields. No. 11 Group just about managed to counter most of these attacks. With the numbers of aircraft involved, it's not surprising that the 15th of

August proved to be the day of the heaviest German losses during the battle. It became known as *"der Schwarze Donnerstag"* – black Thursday.

Dornier Do 17s of 9/KG 76 approach Beachy Head at zero feet en route to bomb Kenley airfield on 18 August 1940, "the Hardest Day" for both sides.

Three days later, both sector airfields at Kenley and Biggin Hill were seriously damaged during massive raids. The 18th of August then became known on both sides of the conflict as "the Hardest Day", simply because both the RAF and the *Luftwaffe* suffered horrific losses. For Fighter Command, this was merely a foretaste of things to come towards the end of August, when the pressure on these southern fighter bases became almost intolerable and experienced pilot losses reached alarming levels.

Hermann Goering called his commanders to his luxurious home, *Carinhall*, 10 miles northeast of Berlin, on the 19th of August for what was effectively a *post mortem* on the sorties conducted over the preceding week. The purpose of the meeting was to modify the organisation of the air units engaged in the attacks against Britain, in particular the fighter units, to take account of their experiences since Eagle Day.

In what was to become a characteristic criticism of the performance of the *Jagdwaffe* units, Goering used this platform to shrug off the lack of effective tactical planning and technical problems that should have been the responsibility of *OKL*, i.e. his own command staff, and point to a lack of aggressiveness on the part of the fighter units and their leaders. The high losses incurred over the previous week across the broad spectrum of aircraft types engaged against Britain were laid at the door of the failure by the fighter units to pursue aggressive tactics and destroy sufficient numbers of British fighters.

In an effort to reinvigorate the *Jagdwaffe* units, Goering instigated across-the-board changes in the fighter units' commanders, replacing many of the older leaders over the days that followed by younger and more aggressive pilots who had demonstrated their qualities over the preceding weeks and months.

Werner Moelders had already been promoted to head JG 51 on the 27th of July, while Adolf Galland became *Kommodore* of JG 26 on the 22nd of August. During the days that followed Wick, Trautloft, Lutzow and Schellmann were among the younger pilots selected for command of various units, with their former, generally older, commanders being moved to other posts away from the Channel front. Operational skill and age were to become the new criteria in selecting *Jagdwaffe* leaders. The recommended maximum age for a *Geschwaderkommodore* became 32, 30 for a *Gruppenkommandeur* and 27 for a *Staffelkapitan*.

During the same meeting, the difficulties experienced by both the *Junkers* Ju 87 *Stuka* dive-bomber and the Bf 110 *Zerstoerer* heavy fighter were acknowledged. The *Stuka* was withdrawn from operations against Britain until RAF Fighter Command was neutralised. Goering then stipulated that his heavy fighters were not to be used as bomber escorts except on operations where the fuel limitations of the Bf 109 threatened the bombers' fighter cover.

Despite some notable successes, the early battles had already shown that where the Bf 110 groups were operating as close escort to slower bomber formations, they could be particularly vulnerable to the more nimble RAF fighters. As the German attacks built up over the following days, the need for increased fighter protection for daylight bombing raids against targets around and to the north of London, meant that the Bf 110s increasingly had to shoulder this burden as the Bf 109 escorts were forced to withdraw somewhere over the capital's outskirts. Paradoxically, the additional Bf 110 losses that were caused by this meant that the heavy fighter groups soon found themselves needing to be escorted by Bf 109 single engine fighters in an effort to stem what were becoming disastrous losses of Goering's favoured *Zerstoerer* units.

Between the 12th and the 18th of August, some 90 Bf 110 heavy fighters had been lost on operations across the Channel. Putting this into context, on Eagle Day itself (13th August 1940), the three *Luftflotten* facing Britain (*Luftflotten 2, 3* and *5*) had available approximately 250 serviceable Bf 110 aircraft, including the fighter-bombers of the fighter-bomber unit, *Erprobungsgruppe 210*. This didn't take into account the heavy fighters then operating as night-fighters in the defence of Germany.

The loss of 90 of these aircraft, some 36% of those available, over six days had served as a salutary warning over the suitability of the *Zerstoerer* units in direct confrontation with Spitfires and Hurricanes over southern England.

These new directives left the fighter unit commanders under no illusion that their task was to hunt and destroy the RAF fighter force in the most effective and aggressive manner they could devise. The new leaders nevertheless found their orders to protect the bomber formations at all costs gave them contradictory aims.

Tactically, both types of German fighter were best suited to flying high above the normal height of the bombers, from where they could identify threats to the bombers and dive to protect them. Being forced to fly close escort to the slower bombers at much lower heights made all the *Jagdwaffe* pilots nervous, since this made them the potentially easy targets for any British fighters that had managed to gain some height advantage. Having to deal with both roles meant that compromises were made that inevitably led to increasing fighter losses as the summer progressed.

Local Casualties 12th - 23rd August 1940

2.   Bf 109 E-1 of JG 52 on 12th August near Selmeston

Despite the poor weather of the preceding few days and early morning mist, the 12th of August became warm and sunny over most of southern England. The start of the German air offensive, *Adlertag* (Eagle Day), had already been delayed by the weather conditions, and had been re-scheduled for the next day. As a prelude to this on the 12th of August, the *Luftwaffe* planned heavy attacks on the south coast, focussing on the radar installations, as well as hitting port facilities and airfields in the area.

While German scientists had been at least a year ahead of their British counterparts in developing radar, the*Luftwaffe* had not integrated radar into its aerial defence umbrella on anything like the scale that Dowding had demanded for Britain. Germany did have a few stations designed to detect aerial attack, but the main military use of this new technology was within the Navy where it was used in naval gunnery targeting. There was also a mobile radar unit east of Calais, used to detect convoy traffic through the Channel.

By this time however, the *Luftwaffe*'s Chief Signals' Officer, General Martini, had developed a fairly shrewd idea that the high radio masts grouped at various locations around Britain's coasts allowed Fighter Command some early warning of the build up of attacking formations. While he was unaware of what role these structures played in Britain's aerial defence mechanism, he argued forcibly with Goering that they should be attacked as a preparatory phase of the main assault. Goering reluctantly agreed to see what the effect was.

Early on the 12th of August, four flights each of four aircraft from the fighter-bomber unit, *Erprobungsgruppe 210* (Experimental or Test Wing 210) were briefed to attack the radar stations at Dover, Dunkirk (Canterbury), Rye and Pevensey.

The Pevensey station, built on the Pevensey Levels around what is now Pylons Farm, was hit by eight 500 kg bombs from one of the flights of Bf 110s, and electricity supplies were cut off for a while. Portable generators succeeded in getting the station back on line later that day, and the radar coverage remained basically unaffected. The other radar sites received varying degrees of damage, but with the masts remaining intact, none were out of service for very long. The apparent lack of damage to these four sites was undoubtedly pivotal to Goering's decision to dismiss Britain's radar network as a worthwhile target.

Leo Zaunbrecher poses with his mechanic in front of his Messerschmitt Bf 109 E-1 with the II. JG 52 unit emblem clearly visible.(MP)

This was one of the first bombing sorties over the British mainland for the fighter-bombers of *Erprobungsgruppe 210*, which had previously been operating against convoy traffic, either in the Channel or off the east coast. While the radar stations picked up the incoming aircraft, their speed identified them as fighters, rather than the bombers that Dowding had instructed his sector controllers to intercept. The rule for fighter incursions was to leave them alone, or send a token force to intercept.

In this case, when Corporal Daphne Griffiths, the duty radar operator at the Rye radar station, reported the approaching aircraft to Fighter Command's filter controller at Bentley Priory, the raid was given an "X" designation, indicating the questionable threat they posed as fighters. When the controller contacted her some minutes later to find out what was going on, she was reported to have primly replied "Your X plot is bombing us!"

Nearer midday, there was a heavy sortie against Portsmouth and Southampton by 63 *Junkers* Ju 88s of KG 51 *Edelweissgeschwader*, escorted by 120 Bf 110 heavy fighters from *Zerstoerergeschwader* (ZG) 2 and ZG 76. An additional top cover escort of some 25 Bf 109s from JG 53 was sent direct to the target area from their bases in northwest France in order to conserve fuel.

The main force crossed the coast near Brighton and proceeded west towards Portsmouth, aiming for the docks as well as the key radar installation at Ventnor. This suffered serious damage to its power supply, and was not back in service for three days, a fact that was concealed from the Germans by sending out dummy radar signals.

The initial part of the raid was intercepted by Hurricanes from Squadrons 145 (Westhampnett) and 257 (Northolt), together with Spitfires from Squadrons 266 (Tangmere) and 152 (Warmwell).

On such long distance daylight raids, the Bf 109s from northwest France soon reached their fuel limits. In order to maintain continuity of fighter escort for the bombers, an additional formation of Bf 109s from JG 52 was sent around midday from their base at Coquelles to rendezvous with the bomber formation on its return leg. Fighter Command strategically placed 615 Squadron's Hurricanes from Biggin Hill between the bomber formation returning from the west and the replacement escort following the Sussex coast westwards to meet them.

II.*Gruppe*/JG 52 lost three aircraft on this sortie, one of these being a Bf 109 E-1 that crash-landed at 1245 hours at Selmeston, near Berwick. This was "Red 14" (*Werk Nummer* 3367) of the 5th *Staffel*, piloted by *Unteroffizier* (Corporal) Leo Zaunbrecher. He became the victim of Pilot Officer J. McClintock, flying a Hurricane of 615 Squadron over the Sussex coast not far from Beachy Head.

Many German pilots attacked over the Channel or southern Britain throughout the Battle of Britain suffered from what has been termed "Spitfire snobbery". Very few recognised that they had been victims of attacks by Hurricanes, even though No. 11 Group operated twice as many Hurricanes as Spitfires. Leo Zaunbrecher may well have been afflicted by this blinkered view, since his preliminary interrogation report by RAF Intelligence indicated that he thought he had been attacked from the rear by a Spitfire at about 19,500 feet. During this encounter, his controls and fuel tank were hit, forcing him to make an emergency landing.

Resting amid the corn stokes of Mays Farm, "Red 14" is examined by British service personnel, the rear fuselage showing clear evidence of the attack that brought the aircraft down. (MP)

He came down in a field which was part of Mays Farm, not far from Selmeston village. Contemporary photos show the crash site between Mays Farm and the railway line, with Stonery Farm on the horizon to the southeast. The pilot was wounded in the shoulder and hospitalised at Princess Alice Hospital in Eastbourne, minus his identity disc that had been taken by one of the local villagers.

Photos taken at the time show the rear section of the Bf 109's fuselage riddled with bullet holes from the machine guns of P/O McClintock's Hurricane. Also prominent is the 5th *Staffel's* unit emblem of the little red devil (*rabatz*) on the port engine cowling, which probably soon became someone else's souvenir of the crash. Various mementoes of this casualty, including some documents donated by Zaunbrecher, are in the inventory of the Kent Battle of Britain Museum at Hawkinge in Kent.

During a later sortie on the same day, P/O McClintock's Hurricane (N2328) overturned on landing at Hawkinge at 2045 hours, but he was unhurt and the aircraft repairable. Sadly, he was later killed in a flying accident on 25th of November 1940, after his squadron had been moved to Scotland for a rest from its operations during the Battle of Britain.

It must have been difficult throughout the Battle of Britain to attribute particular casualties clearly to individual pilots. The speeds at which combat was joined, surprise attacks from the rear, wild attacking and evasive manoeuvres, adrenalin rush and fear must all have made accurate observation a practised skill, with much of the detail perhaps never truly clear. This potential for inaccuracy, understandable though it was, led to both sides vastly over-estimating the aircraft destroyed day by day and confused the circumstances of most actions.

For British pilots, it was frequently complicated when several pilots attacked the same machine, either together or at different times, possibly with each claiming a kill. Documented examples show that some German victims were claimed as separate kills by up to eight individual pilots. Most of the German aircraft brought down should have been obvious from the wreckage scattered around the countryside of the Home Counties, with their crew either dead or taken prisoner of war.

A Hurricane 1 from 615 Squadron landing at Northolt, west of London.

Despite some pilots not having their claims confirmed by Intelligence personnel, it was not unknown for one real German plane loss to be awarded as four separate, confirmed, individual kills, with two other pilots each being awarded a half kill. One real German loss therefore became five. This created an unfortunate, but understandable tendency to overestimate German losses considerably. This explains most of what we now see as the huge disparity between the German losses highlighted on the newspaper placards and subsequent identification of actual losses.

For the *Luftwaffe* fighter pilots, the difficulties of accurately keeping track of British casualties were increased in parallel with the intensity of the air battles. There was no time to watch the fate of aircraft that had been attacked without the risk of collision or attack from an unseen opponent.

It was more difficult for the German pilots to be sure of the outcome of their attacks on British aircraft. Some would be clear from aircraft visibly exploding in mid-air or crashing into the ground with or without their pilots being able to bale out. However, a large number of the RAF fighters that were hit during these battles were able to make a crash-landing on British soil. In these cases, German Intelligence was unable to identify how quickly unwounded pilots could be returned to action, or how many of these aircraft were recovered and repaired.

This introduced an extra complication into the process of German Intelligence evaluation of the deterioration of RAF fighter strength. They had little appreciation of how efficient the maintenance depots in Britain had become in repairing and cannibalising recovered aircraft that had force-landed or crashed.

At the time of the crash-landing of Zaunbrecher's Bf 109, P/O McClintock's combat report described an encounter with a group of five Bf 109s between Beachy Head and Brighton, starting at about 15,000 ft and finishing at 4,000 ft. He was Red 2 in "A" flight, and his combat report reads as follows.

We split up when we met a number of 109s at 15,000 ft. After circling, I attacked a single 109 from the beam. I was diving and he climbing. As I closed, he throttled back. By the time I was in range, his speed appeared to be NIL and I fired one long burst closing to within 50 ft. Almost hitting him, I turned hard left and down, and he disappeared turning right, when I pulled out, he was not in sight, but I am sure he was hit.

During the same action, South African P/O "Dutch" Hugo, DFC was Red 3 of "A" flight, and he described his role in the same action in the day's combat report as follows.

No. 615 Squadron was sent off to patrol Southampton Water and vectored up the coast. Over Beachy Head, we ran into some 109s. Red 1 turned to attack a formation of 5 in line astern; I was Red 3 and attacked the last machine. I fired a short burst and then lost him. A few seconds later, another 109 came past. I fired a short burst of 3-4 seconds, smoke and vapour came from machine. I fired more short bursts and the enemy aircraft went into a very steep dive. At 6,000 ft, he flattened out and I finished my ammunition on him. He landed about 15 miles south of Hastings, and the pilot waved while he was floating. I called the ground base on the R/T and gave his position. Then I landed at Hawkinge to report and have a boat sent out to collect the pilot.

Red 1 of "A" flight also damaged a Bf 109, which was last seen going down vertically on fire, as well as destroying another which crashed into the sea. 615 Squadron's Green section also joined in the action.

The casualty returns of JG 52 show that two other Bf 109s from II.*Gruppe* were missing that day over the Sussex coast, in addition to *Unteroffizier* Zaunbrecher's aircraft. *Unteroffizier* Kern's Bf 109 E-1 failed to return from a sortie over Hastings, with the pilot recorded as killed. Similarly, *Leutnant* Gehlhaar was recorded as missing on the same sortie, with his Bf 109 E-4 shown as lost. There appears to be no record of the rescue of the pilot shot down into sea by P/O Hugo, either by British or German air/sea rescue forces, but it's conceivable that this could have been the unfortunate *Leutnant* Gehlhaar.

During the following two weeks, II.*Gruppe*/JG 52 suffered such heavy losses on the Channel Front that they were withdrawn from their base at Coquelles later in August. Unlike many other *Jagdwaffe* units, they were sent to Germany as a home defence unit in order to give them time to recover from the damage inflicted by the RAF's Spitfires and Hurricanes, with some 30 pilots from JG 52 eventually taken prisoner of war.

3.   Bf 110 D of *Erprobungsgruppe 210* on 15th August near Hooe

The 15th of August was to be the *Luftwaffe's* "Greatest Day", when the full weight of all of its air fleets would be sent against British defences. By the end of the day, once the full impact of the German losses was clear, it became known as *"der schwartze Donnerstag"* – black Thursday. It turned out to be the day when the *Luftwaffe* experienced its heaviest losses of men and machines during the whole of the campaign.

At the end of the day, while returning to France after dive-bombing Croydon Airport some 40 minutes earlier, a twin-engine Bf 110 D fighter-bomber from the *Stab* (Headquarters) flight of *Erprobungsgruppe 210* was shot down around 1900 hours. The German aircraft crash-landed on the marshy fields of School Farm, Hooe, where the pilot, *Leutnant* Karl-Heinz Koch (Group Technical Officer) and his radio operator (*bordfunker*), *Unteroffizier* Rolf Kahl, were captured.

The pilot was unhurt, but his companion had been severely wounded during their flight from Croydon. Koch was eventually sent as a POW to Canada along with several of his unit's comrades also shot down and captured during this sortie. Koch's pet dog, "Grock", named after a popular German comedian of the 1930s, waited in vain back in France for his master's return, and was soon adopted by one of Koch's colleagues in the unit. Rolf Kahl was repatriated to Germany in 1943 due to the severity of his injuries.

Koch's Messerschmitt Bf 110 under guard after landing in the marshy fields of School Farm, Hooe.(CGC)

Koch's Bf 110 (*W. Nr.* 3339) came to a stop slewed across one of the many drainage ditches that criss-cross this area of recovered farmland, not far from Pevensey Marshes on the north eastern side of Waller's Haven. During the landing, the aircraft suffered comparatively minor structural damage, and it was soon camouflaged with netting to prevent its destruction by enemy aircraft and allow RAF Intelligence officers to examine the machine. One of the other aircraft from Koch's unit, which crash-landed on the same mission at Hawkhurst, also suffered comparatively minor damage and was later sent to the U.S. for evaluation.

Leutnant Koch described the aftermath of the raid on Croydon airport after dropping his bomb load and trying to regain all-important height by forming up in a defensive circle (*abwehrkreis*) with his colleagues. This turning formation allowed each crew to provide mutual cover against the attacking Hurricanes of 32 and 111 Squadrons, as they attempted to extricate themselves from their exposed position.

During this circling and climbing, my left engine was hit - presumably by AA - and shortly afterwards my rear gunner was also hit and became unconscious. After reaching about 6,000 feet, I decided to leave this unfriendly area and found myself on my own. My left engine was less than windmilling, and therefore the airspeed was lower than normal; my rear gunner was partly conscious. Approaching the coast west of Hastings, I was suddenly attacked by two fighters without any counter action by my rear gunner. Both engines died immediately. I dived simultaneously to the right to break off from the fighters and looked for a reasonable belly landing field in order to save my rear gunner's life. I crash-landed the aircraft on a wasteland between smaller and larger pools filled with some water and was received by the Home Guard. My rear gunner was taken to hospital, and I was taken by the Police to the Police Station at Hastings. That was the end of my 100th mission.

His fate was attributed to Flight Lieutenant Humphrey ("Humph") a'Becket Russell in a Hurricane of 32 Squadron based at Biggin Hill. Like many RAF fighter squadrons in No. 11 Group during this phase of the Battle of Britain, 32 (The Royal) Squadron was in action from early afternoon until the early evening that day. The intensity of the *Luftwaffe* attacks at this time was a mere foretaste of what was to come later in August and early September.

F/L Russell took off from Biggin Hill at 1845, leading Pilot Officer J. ("Polly") Flinders of 32 Squadron's Training Flight. As they climbed away from Biggin Hill, they saw the German aircraft on their approach to Croydon, but were too low to play any role in preventing that attack, so F/L Russell continued to climb in order to get the sun behind him. Eventually he observed six aircraft about four miles away, returning to the southeast en route back to France. He caught up with this group and dived on the rear aircraft with the sun behind him.

I fired three bursts of one second each and the enemy aircraft hobbled badly and the starboard engine smoked badly. I broke away below and to port and then steep turned and attacked the same enemy aircraft from astern again. I fired three more bursts of one second each and the enemy aircraft turned onto its side, began to smoke very badly and lost height rapidly and I last saw it one mile south of Bexhill turning inland about 1,000 ft off the water. A searchlight site confirm this as having crashed at R.1326. The searchlight site identifies this aircraft as a Me 110.

During fighting over Biggin Hill three days later, F/L Russell's Hurricane (V7363) was hit in the cockpit by a 20 mm cannon shell, but he succeeded in baling out, seriously wounded in the leg, later to be treated at Edenbridge Hospital. His aircraft's crashed remains were subsequently recovered many years later by the London Air Museum, which presented its cockpit clock to F/L Russell in 1979. The Museum has since closed, probably having distributed its exhibits to various establishments around the country.

Separated from F/L Russell during the climb away from Biggin Hill, P/O ("Polly") Flinders also had some success, claiming a Bf 109 destroyed. Only one Bf 109 from *Erprobungsgruppe 210* was lost that evening, this being the Bf 109 E-4/B ("Yellow 3") of *Leutnant* Horst Marx, which crashed near Frant. After dropping his own bomb on Croydon airport, *Lt.* Marx had chosen to escort the Bf 110 of the unit's commander, *Hauptmann* Walter Rubensdoerffer, which had been damaged over Croydon. In doing so, he became the victim of P/O Flinders whose path he crossed. *Lt.* Marx baled out of his aircraft and landed near Frant where he surrendered to local police, joining them in their efforts to find the crash site of Rubensdoerffer's own machine a few miles away. P/O Flinders' combat report makes the following observations.

I took off from Biggin Hill at 18.45 on August 15th in Hurricane N2062 with S/Ldr (actually F/L) Russell. We climbed to 12,000 ft in the direction of Kenley, but on the climb I was left behind. When I was at 12,000 ft, I saw anti-aircraft bursts in the direction of Croydon and, on investigation saw that enemy aircraft had bombed Croydon aerodrome. I flew in that direction and saw two Ju 88s on my right and 3,000 ft above me flying in a SE direction about four miles away. I gave chase and was catching them up when an Me 109 came towards me on the starboard side. I throttled back completely and he passed in front of me into my sights. I fired for about two seconds (at about 100 yards) and a stream of white smoke came from his engine. The aircraft dived towards the ground. I realised he could not get home and continued to chase the bombers. A minute later I saw a parachute open at about 6,000 ft south of Sevenoaks. By now the Ju 88s were about six miles ahead and I was still a long way out of range when I reached the coast. I returned to base.

Many British pilots, both novice and experienced, frequently mistook Bf 110s for bombers such as the *Dornier* Do 17 or Do 215, also twin engine planes with twin fins. The use of the Bf 110 in a dive-bombing role, rather than as a heavy escort fighter, also fostered this regular misidentification of the Bf 110 fighter-bombers as used by *Erprobungsgruppe 210*. Doubtless, P/O Flinders, some distance from the two machines he took to be Ju 88s, focussed on the fact that they had twin engines, rather than noticing that the "Ju 88s" had twin fins rather than the single fin of the Ju 88.

In the early days of the war, most *Luftwaffe* pilots regarded it as a privilege to be posted to the elite units that were equipped with the heavy *Zerstoerer* (destroyer) fighters, units that Goering favoured. His own nephew, *Oberleutnant* Hans-Joachim Goering, flew a Bf 110 as part of the 9th *Staffel* of ZG 76 until he was shot down over Portland on the 11th of July, much to the anguish of his uncle.

A Messerschmitt Bf 110 D-0 of the 1st Staffel, Erprobungsgruppe 210 waits fully-loaded. Clearly visible are the four 7.9 mm MG 17 machine guns in the upper nose, with the two troughs for the 20 mm MGFF cannons under the nose. The unit insignia can be seen under the windscreen, halfway down the fuselage. (ECC)

Erprobungsgruppe 210 was uniquely allowed some freedom of action in the pinpoint bombing raids that were to become their speciality. Many of the remaining *Zerstoerer* units ended up in the Battle of Britain as close escorts to bomber formations, limitations that ultimately cancelled out most of the positive qualities of this heavy machine.

The Bf 110 was more suited to diving attacks from above, using its relatively high speed and formidable forward armament of four machine guns and two cannon. Before the fall of Dunkirk, they had been free to use these aggressive attacking manoeuvres, rather than being forced into dog fighting with more nimble machines. In close escort, the lack of manoeuvrability caused by the size and weight of the aircraft cancelled out most of these advantages. Forced to keep close contact with the bomber formations, these units lost the ability to use their advantages since they could only react to the British attacks. They were under no illusion that they could not abandon the bombers.

Units equipped with the Bf 110 were to have the heaviest casualty records of any other part of the *Luftwaffe* during the Battle of Britain, and this was amply demonstrated on the 15th of August 1940, when some 24 of the *Zerstoerer* fighters were lost, and several more returned to base damaged, with wounded on board.

Erprobungsgruppe 210 had been formed as an experimental test unit to develop tactics for the use of fighter aircraft in the role of fighter-bombers independent of separate fighter cover. The aim was to provide the German armed forces with a pinpoint bombing cadre to supplement the slower *Junkers* Ju 87 (*Stuka*) dive-bomber. Personnel and aircraft were drawn from several different units, some previously operating Bf 110s, some Bf 109s, and others from conventional dive-bombing units, normally equipped with the *Stuka*.

Walter Rubensdoerffer, the Swiss-born commander of Erpobungsgruppe 210, whose grasp of fighter-bomber tactics allowed the unit to have an impact that far outweighed either its size or the losses it suffered. (CGC)

After the blitzkrieg in Europe, ending in the fall of France and the British evacuation from Dunkirk, the suitability of the *Stuka* for operations across the English Channel was justifiably questioned. After some success on Channel convoy attacks during the early part of the Battle of Britain, their vulnerability was amply demonstrated as RAF fighters frequently decimated formations that had insufficient escorting fighters. As a result, most of these units were withdrawn from this sector, having suffered heavy losses. Attacks by RAF fighters on unescorted *Stuka* formations were gleefully described as "*Stuka* parties", and all the RAF fighter pilots wanted to gate crash.

This unique unit was also assigned the task of evaluating the planned replacement for the Bf 110, a new twin-engine, multi-role heavy fighter, the *Messerschmitt* Me 210. However, in its early deliveries for *Luftwaffe* trials, the new aircraft fell far short of the standards required for it to enter operational service, and it did not do so until much later in 1941. Although the Me 210 continued to be produced until 1944, it was never delivered in significant numbers (75 - 95 machines per year) and remains one of Willy Messerschmitt's notable failures. However, *Erprobungsgruppe 210* never deployed this machine in combat in 1940, despite the aircraft's model number forming part of the unit's name.

During the comparatively short span of its operational life (1st July 1940 - 24th April 1941), the unit gained a much-deserved reputation for daring and skill. Frequently during the Battle of Britain, its aircraft were in the forefront of the conflict, performing raids on shipping, airfields, radar installations and other pinpoint targets.

It is perhaps fortunate for Britain that none of the German commanders at the time appreciated earlier in the summer of 1940 how the tactics employed by *Erprobungsgruppe 210* might have changed the progress of the battle if other *Zerstoerer* groups had adopted them early in the summer of 1940.

With only one such wing, the successful raids that this unit frequently conducted were dangerous and damaging. Had other Bf 110 groups converted their aircraft to carry a bomb load and followed similar tactics on a continuous basis from the early part of the summer, the disruption to the British air defence system could have been much worse. Fortunately for Britain, the increasing demands by the German bomber units for greater numbers of visible, i.e. close, fighter escorts effectively prevented this.

Even if such an expanded fighter-bomber role for the Bf 110 had been identified early on, the *Luftwaffe* did not have sufficient overall fighter strength to put such plans into practice. German industry simply did not have the capacity to produce enough aircraft to keep pace with operational losses since it was not organised to cater for a long war of attrition.

Erprobungsgruppe 210 ground crew position a 500 kg bomb on the starboard bomb rack under the fuselage of one of the unit's Bf 110s. (ECC)

Towards the end of September, as daylight raids by *Dornier*, *Heinkel* and *Junkers* bombers tailed off, some *Zerstoerer* units remaining on the Channel front converted some of their aircraft to carry similar bomb loads to the aircraft of *Erprobungsgruppe 210*. ZG 26 regularly operated a *schwarm* of Bf 110 fighter-bombers from late October 1940, but both these and the *Jagdwaffe's* Bf 109s that had by then been converted for a similar purpose were employed mainly in high altitude bombing missions, where accuracy was an understandable sacrifice.

By late autumn, the need for daylight fighter escort of bomber formations had by then tailed off and, as with the single engine fighter units, *Luftwaffe* High Command switched a proportion of the heavy fighter units into the fighter-bomber role, more successfully pioneered by *Erprobungsgruppe 210*. The earlier need for fighters as bomber escorts from August onwards prevented this change of tactics for the Bf 110 units until after the turning point of the battle in the early autumn.

In the middle of August 1940, *Erprobungsgruppe 210* used Denain, near Valenciennes, east of Arras, as its home base. On offensive operations, the group would leave Denain at first light for one of the forward airfields on the north French coast, operating from there during the day, and generally returning to Denain in the evening. From the 9th of August, the group used Calais-Marck as their forward base, rather than St. Omer-Arques, which they had used earlier.

The unit operated a *Stab* (Staff) flight and two *Staffeln* equipped with Bf 110 fighter-bombers, and one further *Staffel* equipped with single engine Bf 109s, modified so that they could also carry a small bomb load and participate in the pin point raids that became the unit's trade mark. These were Bf 109 E-4/Bs, equipped with centreline racks under the fuselage, enabling them to carry a 250 kg bomb.

At this point in the Battle of Britain, RAF Intelligence was apparently unaware of this change to the Bf 109's tactical flexibility, assuming all were operating in the normal fighter role. RAF Intelligence Report A.I.1. (k) No. 268/1940, prepared after the unit's raid on Croydon in mid August, underlines that the Bf 109s operated by the unit's 3rd *Staffel* were normal fighter versions of this aircraft, intended for use as escorts for the Bf 110 fighter-bombers.

Messerschmitt Bf 109 E-4/B loaded with a 250 kg bomb.

Apart from the one Bf 109 that was completely destroyed crashing near Frant on the 15th of August, *Erprobungsgruppe 210* lost none of the Bf 109s operating in its 3rd *Staffel* over British soil until much later in the autumn. It was mid September before RAF crash investigators were able to examine a Bf 109 fighter-bomber that had force-landed near Ashford in Kent. This was a machine from another unit, the 6th *Staffel Lehrgeschwader 2*, which was later to join in operations alongside *Erprobungsgruppe 210*.

As the autumn began, the use of the Bf 109 in this *Jabo* role in other fighter groups would become much more widespread. For both RAF Intelligence and the *Luftwaffe* High Command itself, the use of Bf 110 aircraft as fighter-bombers by *Erprobungsgruppe 210* should have been an earlier wake-up call to the pinpoint bombing potential of these heavy fighters.

The raid on Croydon is interesting for a number of reasons. The early weather forecast over the Channel and the south of Britain had not been encouraging for flying operations. Goering took the opportunity to call his commanders together to berate them for their apparent inability to back up his boast to Hitler that the RAF would be destroyed in a week. The weather cleared by mid-morning and II. *Fliegerkorps* launched some the biggest raids to date with 1,120 aircraft attacking airfields mainly in the south and southeast but also on the east coast.

Erprobungsgruppe 210 performed at least two bombing missions on the 15th of August, possibly more. They may have been behind a raid on Manston, although the attacking aircraft were tentatively identified as Bf 110s from ZG 76, even though there seems little evidence that any other Bf 110 unit operated this aircraft as fighter-bombers at this early stage.

They had attacked Manston the day before, when they had lost two aircraft to anti aircraft fire, but it's difficult to confirm an attack by this group on Manston on the 15th of August. They certainly bombed Martlesham Heath airfield to some effect at about 1510 hours. Despite being engaged by Hurricanes of both 1 and 17 Squadrons on their flight back to France, no German casualties were recorded as a result of this raid. The same was not to be the case during their last raid of the day, the attack on Croydon airfield.

Around 1820 hours, a small formation of *Dornier* 17s and escorting Bf 109s crossed the coast heading for Biggin Hill, where they were intercepted by Hurricanes of 32 Squadron and Spitfires of 610 Squadron. While the fighters attacked the escorting Bf 109s, the bombers continued towards their target, but hit West Malling in error. As the German formation broke off to return home, 32 Squadron decided to chase the bombers, but as they started to do so, they were vectored back towards Biggin Hill. From their relatively high altitude, they were able to see an ominous pall of smoke over south London.

Fourteen Bf 110 and eight Bf 109 fighter-bombers had crossed the coast near Dungeness, slightly north of the *Dornier* group. They either remained undetected until too late as they flew towards London or, with their high speed identifying them as fighters, they were ignored by the sector controllers. They were escorted by Bf 109s of JG 52 but, for reasons that have never been clearly understood, the JG 52 escort turned back for home.

This may have been because of the usual fuel and range limitations experienced by Bf 109 pilots, but it's also possible that the fighters lost sight of the fighter-bombers in the reduced visibility, caused by the evening summer haze and the setting sun. They had been flying only 200 metres above the fighter-bomber formation, a vulnerable position to maintain in deteriorating visibility with increasing risks of collision.

Flying westwards into the setting sun with an early evening ground haze also seems to have confused *Gruppenkommandeur Hauptmann* Walter Rubensdoerffer's sense of position. *Oberleutnant* Otto Hintze, the 3rd *Staffel's* leader, was reported to have heard Rubensdoerffer asking quizzically "*Are we over land or sea? I'm going down.*" To solve the question he had decided to lose height just as the group were passing over Croydon, Kenley's satellite airfield.

The Hurricanes of 111 Squadron, based at Croydon, had meanwhile been scrambled some 30 minutes before the Bf 110s reached the South London airfield, giving them ample time to gain sufficient height to dive on the German aircraft.

Since Rubensdoerffer was one of the casualties of the mission, it's impossible to confirm why Croydon, rather than the intended more southerly target of Kenley, was attacked. It's possible that, having lost his Bf 109 escort group, he was worried by the threat from the two approaching squadrons of Hurricanes and decided to drop the bomb load on the nearest airfield and regain maximum manoeuvrability to help them escape back to France. *Leutnant* Koch's later interrogation suggested that he, at least, had become aware the formation was attacking Croydon rather than Kenley as he dived on the airfield from 9,000 feet.

After dropping their bombs from around 2,400 feet, the Bf 110s adopted their standard climbing defensive circle (*abwehrkreis*). Hurricanes from 32 Squadron arrived from the east and attacked the 3rd *Staffel's* Bf 109s, which by then had also dropped their bombs. Both Bf 109s and Bf 110s then ran for the coast, dodging fire from the pursuing Hurricanes but, of the fourteen Bf 110s on the raid, six are brought down, as well as one of the Bf 109s.

Rubensdoerffer's own machine was damaged in the melee over Croydon by gunfire from various Hurricanes, and his radio operator, *Obergefreiter* Ludwig Kretzer, was either killed or seriously injured. While crossing the Kent/Sussex border en route to the coast, his aircraft was attacked for the final time by Pilot Officer Duckenfield of 501 Squadron near Tunbridge Wells. It crashed in flames nearby at Bletchinglye Farm, Rotherfield, with the loss of both crewmen.

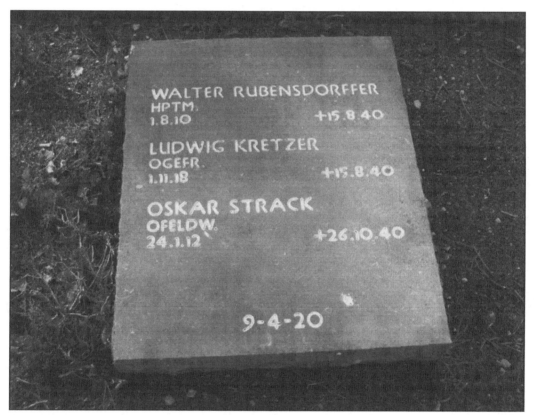

A simple memorial stone in the German War Graves Commission cemetery at Cannock Chase marks the final resting place for Walter Rubensdoerffer and Ludwig Kretzer, still together after their fatal crash on 15 August 1940.

The raid inflicted serious damage on Croydon airfield, and the surrounding civilian areas suffered heavily. The H.E. Rollason Aircraft Works was destroyed, the British N.S.F. factory was severely damaged, as well as other industrial facilities in the area. The majority of the casualties, however, were from the civilian areas outside the aerodrome's perimeter, where some 62 civilians were killed in the collateral damage caused by the bombing.

Walter Rubensdoerffer had violated, albeit unwittingly, Hitler's directive that civilian targets in London and its suburbs were not to be attacked except under his personal orders. Hitler was furious when he heard the reports of the attack. He remained convinced that Britain could be manoeuvred into a peaceful settlement, and he wanted to avoid heavy civilian casualties, particularly in London, in the hope that this might gain support for such peace overtures among the British public. Despite this, Rubensdoerffer was posthumously awarded the Knight's Cross four days later in recognition of his skilful leadership of this special unit of fighter-bombers.

In hitting Croydon rather than Kenley, and incurring heavy civilian casualties in this area of south London, Rubensdoerffer's actions helped to lay the foundations for subsequent British bombing missions aimed at the German capital, Berlin. Following the Croydon raid and a night raid on the 24th of August, which hit both central London and the docklands, RAF Bomber Command was ordered to bomb Berlin on the night of 25/26th of August.

4.   Bf 110 C of ZG 2 on 16th August in Meads, Eastbourne

Like many warm summer days in 1940, the 16th of August was perfect for flying operations, with high temperatures, clear skies and some haze over the Channel. After the hectic action of the preceding four days, the RAF's fighter pilots were already beginning to wish for weather conditions that would allow them more time to rest and recuperate between missions. The weather was set to deteriorate later, but this change was still several days away.

During the day, the *Luftwaffe* launched some 1,700 sorties against various targets in Britain. As the day drew to a close, a formation of *Heinkel* He 111 bombers from KG 55 was detected coming across the Channel. Together with an escort of Bf 110s from ZG 2, ZG 26 and ZG 76, they were heading for airfields west of London around Heathrow. The German formation managed to get well inland to the Surrey/Sussex borders before being intercepted by Hurricanes from 1 Squadron (Northolt) and 615 Squadron (Kenley), as well as Spitfires from 610 Squadron (Biggin Hill). Four of the bombers were claimed destroyed in the ensuing action, as well as a number of Bf 110s, with several of the heavy fighters also being badly damaged.

Taking advantage of the August sunshine, Mrs. Ockenden was pushing her two-year old son, Michael, along the Eastbourne seafront in his pushchair when she was alarmed by the sounds of an aerial battle close overhead. Maternal caution persuaded her to rush back to the shelter of their nearby Meads Street home. As she and her son arrived at their door, they were greeted by the sounds of an aircraft's screaming descent, with debris crashing into nearby houses and gardens.

Michael Ockenden was later to play what was for me a crucial role in fleshing out some of the detail surrounding the action that caused this aircraft to crash so close to his childhood home. 40 years later, after some assiduous research into the backgrounds of the various characters who played a role in the unfolding events of that day in the summer of 1940, Michael Ockenden published an article in the August 1980 issue of "Sussex Life" entitled "Black Friday", describing this incident. I thank him and "Sussex Life" for allowing me to embroider my own research into this incident with the greater detail he uncovered, lending a more human perspective to my account of the day's events.

The aircraft that Mrs. Ockenden and her son had heard in its last agonised moments before impact had started the day at Guyancourt airfield near Paris. This was the base for II.*Gruppe*/ZG 2, one of the heavy fighter groups which had already been escorting bomber missions against targets in southern Britain.

Recently-promoted Ernst Hollekamp, a 31-year old Bavarian ex-policeman, was not flying his usual aircraft on this mission. For this late afternoon sortie, *Hauptmann* (Flight Lieutenant) Hollekamp and his *bordfunker*, *Feldwebel* (Flight Sergeant) Richard Schurk, were flying *"Gustav-Ludwig"(A2+GL)*, the ill-fated aircraft that crashed in the Meads district of Eastbourne. It carried on its fuselage a yellow "G", identifying the individual aircraft, with the remaining letters painted black, identifying it as belonging to the 6th *Staffel* of II.*Gruppe*/ZG 2. This group had been formed at the end of June 1940 from I.*Gruppe* /ZG 52. The new *Gruppe* used the unit emblem and the *Staffel* identification letters of that earlier formation, contrary to normal practice where the 6th *Staffel* identification letter would have been "P" instead of "L" as in the case of *"Gustav-Ludwig"*

As they returned to France, the German formation was pursued by groups of Hurricanes and Spitfires, suffering a number of losses. At least three of the bombers were brought down over the southern counties, as well as some of the escorting Bf 110s.

Messerschmitt Bf 110s from the 6th Staffel / ZG 2 prepare for take-off. The aircraft in the middle foreground appears to be either the aircraft that crashed in Meads or a similar machine with the individual aircraft letter "C" rather than "G".

Various reports from both RAF and *Luftwaffe* records, supplemented by local police records, point to Hollekamp's aircraft being the victim of an attack over the South Downs by Flying Officer Harold N. E. Salmon in a Hurricane from 1 Squadron based at Northolt.

Harold "Sammy" Salmon had learned to fly with the Royal Air Force Volunteer Reserve (RAFVR) in 1933 and was called up at the outbreak of war in September 1939. He joined 1 Squadron in March 1940 and, since this unit was one of the first squadrons to be sent to the defence of France and the Low Countries, this is where he had his first encounters with the *Luftwaffe*. He remained with the squadron throughout the summer of 1940, claiming the destruction of this particular Bf 110, as well as a probable Bf 109 some weeks earlier.

His was a combat record that was perhaps typical of many RAF fighter pilots during the Battle of Britain, where actual combat claims were a far cry from the level of many "aces" on both sides of the conflict. This is neither a reflection on "Sammy" Salmon's skills as a pilot, nor on his contribution to the efforts made by all RAF fighter pilots during the battle. It's merely a reflection of the opportunities presented to him, and others like him, during the sorties in which they were involved over that summer.

It's clear from the recollections of a number of the higher scoring British fighter pilots who survived the war that there were generally two groups of fighter pilots in Fighter Command. There were the high scorers for whom the challenges of aerial combat suited their underlying hunter/killer instincts. Then there were the others who were more observers than active participants.

F/O Salmon's combat report for the 16th of August described a Bf 110 destroyed during his sortie at 1715 hours, closely matching the time for Hollekamp's crash.

I was Green 2 and Squadron 1. I did not stay with the Squadron for the first attack as I was a little way behind so I climbed to 22,000 ft and then dived on the last section of the bomber formation but a Me 110 came beneath me so I fired a short burst at it and saw the port engine immediately stop and it went into a vertical dive out of control, F/O Matthews confirms this. I continued my dive and went into some cloud as 3 Me 110s attacked me from astern. I continued my dive through the cloud and circling to find my position (and) landed there as I was on my reserve tank.

The aerodrome was Redhill and after re-fuelling and being bombed by a single Do 17, I took off again and landed at Northolt at about 1830.

His description of the port engine stopping during his attack later produced an interesting series of comments to Michael Ockenden from former *Leutnant* Stix, who had been flying another Bf 110 from 6/ZG 2 on the same mission.

Local Home Guard soldiers guard the wreckage of Hollekamp's aircraft in the grounds behind Aldro School. (TRB)

Stix was one of the *Luftwaffe's* more experienced Bf 110 pilots, having been an instructor at the Operational Training Unit at Werneuchen. His skills made him one of the few pilots able to put this heavy aircraft into a violent evasive manoeuvre that was claimed to allow the aircraft surprisingly to evade even the nimble Spitfire. Whilst strictly forbidden for safety reasons, this dangerous course of action involved stopping the port engine and at the same time opening up the other engine at full throttle. This threw the aircraft into a terrifying spinning descent under pressure from the torque of the one engine, with gravitational forces that potentially threatened the integrity of the aircraft's structure, particularly the comparatively delicate tail-plane.

German pilots of both the Bf 110 and the Bf 109 frequently used a diving escape when under attack from either Hurricanes or Spitfires, both powered by the Rolls Royce Merlin power-plant with its float carburettor. Until corrected later in the war, this feature of the British fighters' design had the unsettling habit of momentarily cutting out in a rapid diving descent, as gravity temporarily starved the engine of fuel. With the German aircrafts' fuel injected Daimler Benz engines, this was not a problem for their pilots, who could gain precious seconds of distance until the British pilots began to learn to roll inverted as they dived, thereby minimising the problems with fuel supply.

The manoeuvre outlined by *Leutnant* Stix appears to be a dangerous variation of this diving escape while under attack. F/O Samson's description of the port engine suddenly stopping, followed by an apparently uncontrolled descent, could certainly be interpreted as the result of Ernst Hollekamp going into this evasive manoeuvre. Equally, it could also have been the result of Samson's attacking burst of machine gun fire but, in either case, the outcome was fatal for both the German pilot and his gunner.

At the time of his discussion with Michael Ockenden in the late 1970s, Stix was a retired senior officer from the post-war *Luftwaffe*, having survived the war as a prisoner of war. He had been able to recall the late afternoon mission on the 16th of August 1940, as well as Ernst Hollekamp who had been a former pupil for conversion training to fly the heavy Bf 110. While he felt Hollekamp and Schurk made a good team, they had significantly less experience than himself or the *Gruppenkommandeur* of ZG 2, *Major* Harry Carl from Dresden, a personal friend.

The implication of these comments is that, if Hollekamp had frantically decided on this forbidden manoeuvre to avoid the stream of .303 inch machine gun fire from Salmon's Hurricane, once he had started on this spinning descent, he would probably not have had the experience to neutralise the spin and regain level, controlled flight. As such an uncontrolled descent progressed, the spin would have become more violent and would have risked structural failure of the airframe.

While this may be only one of the possible reasons for the crash of the heavy fighter, those in the vicinity on the ground all described the screaming howl of the falling aircraft as it broke through the clouds "like a falling leaf".

Richard Schurk managed to bale out and parachuted into the sea some 200 yards from the promenade. Despite being visible from the shore, he drowned as he was pulled under by his parachute, his body later being washed ashore. For Ernst Hollekamp, his own parachute was to play an important role in the immediate future, although not in the function for which it had been designed.

The stricken aircraft with Ernst Hollekamp still in the cockpit broke up somewhere over the Royal Eastbourne Golf course, scattering debris over a large part of Upper Meads, with the bulk of the wreckage falling in the grounds behind Aldro School, Darley Road, now also part of the University of Brighton. The unfortunate pilot was thrown from his violently-disintegrating aircraft. It appears unclear whether he had been killed by the fire from "Sammy" Salmon's Hurricane or whether he was killed on impact with the gable roof of Hillbrow in Gaudick Road, now part of the University of Brighton.

Eastbourne Fire Brigade's Pat Short, then a Sub-Officer and later to become Eastbourne's Chief Fire Officer, was one of those sent to the roof of Hillbrow to remove Ernst Hollekamp's body. Not perhaps realising the purpose of the "D"-shaped release ring on the pilot's parachute harness, he chose to tie off the rope with which he planned to lower the body to the ground onto this seemingly-useful attachment. The result was that as his rope and the "D" ring took the weight of the descending body, Hollekamp's parachute deployed and the body dropped, drawing much attention to the spectacle.

Pat Short kept the "D" ring as a souvenir for many years until the early 1960s, when Frau Annelies Hollekamp, the pilot's widow, visited her husband's grave not long before the remains of both pilot and gunner were exhumed for reburial at the German War Graves Commission cemetery at Cannock Chase in Staffordshire. By a curious quirk of fate, while taking a taxi from the railway station to the cemetery, she discovered that the driver knew Pat Short and he later took Frau Hollekamp to meet the fireman at his Cavendish Avenue home. The "D" ring was given to the visiting widow in memory of her husband and so it returned to her Munich home.

The grave marker of Ernst Hollekamp and Richard Schurk shows their final resting place at Cannock Chase after their fateful encounter with 1 Squadron Hurricanes on 16 August 1940 over Eastbourne.

Many years later in 1977, she was visited at her home by 39-year old Michael Ockenden during his own researches into this incident. Annelies Hollekamp showed him the "D" ring, as well as one or two other souvenirs of her late husband's *Luftwaffe* flying career.

The two exchanged Christmas cards for some years until one year when Michael Ockenden received not a Christmas card but a parcel from Germany. Annelies Hollekamp had passed away, and her relatives found little use for the memorabilia of her husband's short flying career. They had consigned these items to a skip until someone recalled the Englishman and his interest in Ernst

Hollekamp. This much-travelled "D" ring is now in Michael Ockenden's possession. This was not the only item he had from the crash on the 16th of August 1940. At the time, his Grandfather had mounted one or two of the instruments that had been gathered from the aircraft's debris onto the dashboard of his treasured Tri-ang pedal car, probably much to the envy of other local children.

"Sammy" Salmon stayed with 1 Squadron until October 1940 with no further credited kills, then being posted to 229 Squadron and later becoming a flying instructor at South Cerney, near Cirencester. He left the RAF in October 1941, but served with the Air Transport Auxiliary between January 1942 and the end of 1943 when, as Captain Salmon, he was lost with his crew while ferrying a B-25 Mitchell twin-engine bomber over the Atlantic.

Ernst Hollekamp and Richard Schurk were not the only *Luftwaffe* casualties that afternoon. *Leutnant* Stix' friend and the leader of ZG 2, *Gruppenkommandeur* Harry Carl, also died with his gunner while attempting a crash-landing near St. Aubin in France, after limping back across the Channel in his badly-damaged aircraft. One of "Sammy" Salmon's 1 Squadron colleagues, Flying Officer Matthews, also claimed a Bf 110 during this sortie, his victim going down in flames over the south coast, as did Flight Lieutenant Pete Brothers from 32 Squadron, whose victim was thought to have crashed in the Channel. From the escorting heavy fighter units that day, a total of seven Bf 110 aircraft were listed as either destroyed or missing.

Sadly, it was not only German aircrew that perished in the Eastbourne area that evening. Samuel Henman, a cheerful and kindly man who had served with the Royal Engineers during World War One, had left his Eshton Road home earlier that day to work with his colleagues, Frank Edwards and Harry White. They were working on salvage collection round the town for the war effort, collecting scrap and other material that could be put to good use. By late afternoon, he and his workmates were in Hampden Park and, on hearing the aerial battle going on not far overhead, they decided to shelter from falling debris and shrapnel under the bed of their Corporation lorry.

Around 1720 hours, fleeing *Luftwaffe* bombers, anxious to speed their return to France, released a string of some two-dozen 50 kg bombs, which straddled the Hampden Park area. One of the bombs fell six feet away from Henman's Corporation lorry outside No. 2 Freeman Avenue, igniting its petrol tank.

His two colleagues were killed outright, but Samuel Henman suffered terrible burns and died later that night in hospital. For many understandably-irate local residents, the bombs dropped in Hampden Park and the aircraft that crashed in Meads were inextricably linked, with some assuming that Hollekamp's aircraft was the bomber that had released the bombs. This was a readily-understandable example of wartime confusion and misconception.

Leutnant Stix managed to land back at Guyancourt unharmed, soon to learn the fate of his friend Harry Carl, as well as the loss of Ernst Hollekamp and Richard Schurk. He continued to fly bomber escort missions with the 6th *Staffel* of ZG 2 until three weeks later when his own aircraft was shot down during another sortie over London on the fateful 7th of September 1940. He was wounded and taken prisoner of war that evening when his aircraft crashed at Little Burstead in Essex, where his gunner, *Gefreiter* Hetz, was killed.

Airfields on the edge: 12th August - 6th September

As the battle continued, the end of August and the early part of September saw both the tempo and scale of the *Luftwaffe* assault on the fighter stations of No. 11 Group intensified.

Following the initial heavy attacks on the southeast's airfields up to the 18th of August, weather conditions deteriorated and did not encourage the same high level of operations. While not inactive, the days leading up to the 24th of August were therefore comparatively quiet, but it was not to stay that way for long. After the command changes within the *Jagdwaffe* units ordered by Goering during the conference at *Carinhall* on the 19th of August, this poor weather allowed the German fighter units to adjust to the new command structure. With younger and more aggressive leaders in charge, the remainder of August and early September allowed the *Luftwaffe* to show how much damage they could do to Fighter Command.

From the 24th of August, the tempo of the attacks was stepped up as the weather improved, with the focus for the heaviest attacks concentrating on No. 11 Group's airfields in the southeast. Goering's offhand dismissal of the radar sites as worthwhile targets had virtually guaranteed their continued operation. Some further attacks were made against individual radar sites, but there was little concerted effort made to degrade their effectiveness.

As an additional bonus, German planning staff had still not recognised the pivotal role that No. 11 Group's sector stations played in controlling the reactions of Fighter Command to incoming raids. Nobody on the other side of the Channel realised that it was through the local control of the sector stations that Group Headquarters' decisions were channelled on which squadrons to scramble against individual *Luftwaffe* attacks. On balance, it seems unlikely that anyone in the *Luftwaffe's Abteilung 5* knew that these sector control rooms even existed, and even if they did, the feeling was that the activities of the fighter squadrons were insulated from those of their neighbours, rather than coordinated through their sector station.

The *Luftwaffe* had been intent on progressively moving its target focus from the coast towards the London outskirts as the days passed following *Adlertag*. Apart from Tangmere, No. 11 Group's sector stations were all located on the outskirts of London, so it was not until the final days of August that these sector stations suffered serious damage at the hands of the *Luftwaffe* bombers, this also being delayed by the bad weather of the previous few days.

Biggin Hill was the target of six raids over three days at the end of August, and by early-September, six out of the seven sector airfields in No. 11 Group were seriously damaged. At various times throughout this period, several of these were declared non-operational for periods while bomb damage, both to the airfield's surface, as well as the communications and control facilities, was repaired. Of the sector stations that effectively translated control from No. 11 Group Headquarters to unit level, only Tangmere and Kenley were operational at one point, the remainder having fallen victim to waves of attacks that did not allow them fully to recover.

Forward airfields, like Manston in Kent, were even more at risk, even though their role was not as central to the defence mechanism as the sector stations. In addition to the regular bombing attacks that all the airfields in the southeast were being subjected to, airfields like Manston, situated overlooking the Channel on this exposed part of the Kent coast, were at greater risk from German fighters coming in low over the sea and strafing the airfield without warning. This vulnerability led to Manston's role during the next few weeks being downgraded to a refuelling and emergency airfield, rather than a forward base for operations.

It was apparent that no-one in the *Luftwaffe* had any understanding of how Britain's air defence mechanism worked, and how pivotal yet vulnerable were the controller's operations rooms at each sector station. With Goering having rejected the radar stations' masts as being of any real significance, it was these operations rooms that could have become RAF Fighter Command's Achilles heel. Instead of being located in deep underground bunkers, as the *Luftwaffe* might have believed had it been aware of them at all, these control rooms were mostly single storey buildings located above ground at each sector airfield, with many protected simply by sandbags. Their critical importance, however, was that they translated the input of radar and the Observer Corps into operational orders for Hurricanes and Spitfires to intercept incoming raiders.

Hermann Goering discusses the role of the Jagdwaffe in defending the bombing assault on Britain with two of his recently-promoted fighter commanders. On the left is Werner Moelders of JG 51 and on the right, Adolf Galland of JG 26. (ECC)

If a number of these rooms at different sector stations could have been taken out at the same time, it would have created a hole in Britain's air defence network that in all probability could not have been repaired swiftly enough to avoid further more permanent damage to the whole structure. Lack of understanding was the key to this failing, amplified by Goering's own instruction that individual airfields were not to be the target of consecutive raids, itself a curious error. Had all of the south's sector stations been targeted two or three times each day over a continuous period of days, the effects on fighter control would have been disastrous. Despite some individual control rooms being temporarily put out of action either through fortuitous bomb damage or cutting of power or telephone lines, when this did happen, the direction of the squadrons it controlled was switched to nearby sector stations until repairs were made.

The *Luftwaffe's* medium bombers rarely bombed from less than 15,000 feet and did not have precision bombsights to allow accurate target acquisition from that height. Early German intelligence reports are thought to have been the basis of this apparent reluctance to mount low level bombing sorties. British airfields were believed to have been protected by roughly twice the number of light anti aircraft guns than was actually the case. German light anti aircraft defences around their own airfields had demonstrated their lethal effectiveness against British bombing raids and the conclusion was that the British airfields would have similarly-effective defences against low level attacks.

Dornier Do 17 medium bombers usually operated in groups of three aircraft to maximise mutual support from their defensive armament. This picture gives a good impression of how exposed the crew were from frontal attack within the largely plexiglass nose section.

Persuaded therefore to bomb from 15,000 - 18,000 feet to minimise losses from anti aircraft fire, the best they could hope for was saturation damage to runways, hangars, personnel, buildings and any aircraft on the ground. Blowing up hangars, fuel dumps and aircraft on the ground was much more visually impressive than hitting inconspicuous wooden buildings, even if they could have been identified as the critical weak points they actually were.

The effectiveness of surprise, low-level bombing attacks by specialist groups such as *Erprobunggruppe 210* had been amply demonstrated during the early days of the German air offensive against convoys and coastal targets. However, as the focus of attacks moved further inland to the sector airfields mostly on the outskirts of London, it became understandably more difficult to achieve the element of surprise, largely due to the need for the attacking formation to fly 10 -15 minutes over the populated south of England before reaching its target.

As the 9th *Staffel* of KG 76 had discovered on the 18th of August, planning low-level bombing attacks on airfields such as Kenley was relatively easy, but the problem was disguising the intended target if it was that far into the Home Counties. The Observer Corps post at Beachy Head reported the group crossing the coast at close to zero feet, clearly heading northwest towards Kenley. The *Dorniers* of KG 76 still had roughly 40 miles to go before reaching their target and by the time they reached the Kenley area, the airfield's local air defences were on alert, waiting for the bombers to appear. Had the element of surprise been in the *Luftwaffe's* favour, the result could have been completely different. As it was, without the benefit of surprise, of the nine *Dorniers* that attacked Kenley that day, four were destroyed, two suffered serious damage and the remaining three all suffered minor damage.

This is not to say that the German bombing tactics were always unproductive. During raids on the 30th of August, one of the German bombs severed the main electricity grid, putting the whole of Kent's radar network out of action and punching a vulnerable hole in Britain's defence umbrella.

Unaware of what they had done, the *Luftwaffe* was unable to take significant advantage of this. The next morning, Biggin Hill was hit by another low-level attack by KG 76, which not only succeeded in cutting the recently-repaired telephone lines, but also knocked out this sector station's vital operations room.

Rather through good fortune than good planning, the *Luftwaffe* had succeeded, however fleetingly, in taking out one of the more important elements of Dowding's command and control system. Other sector stations took over Biggin Hill's role, repairs were made and, the next day, Biggin Hill's operations room was again back in action, relocated to one of the village shops. Regular successes on this scale for the *Luftwaffe* could have radically changed the progress of the next few days.

Still unaware of the existence of the sector stations' operations rooms, let alone how to locate them, German *OKL* focussed on the destruction of Fighter Command, if not through losses incurred in air combat, then through bomb damage to the fighter bases and strategic targeting of aircraft production facilities.

An aerial view of Biggin Hill airfield under attack. The dotted white lines show the explosions of some of the bombs dropped by German bombers.

British fighter production during June, July and August averaged over 470 new machines each month, up till then more than sufficient to keep pace with losses. However, over the ten day period from the 8th - 18th of August, 188 aircraft were lost with only 153 new machines leaving the assembly lines. This made the aircraft losses during the end of August and early September more difficult to replace as quickly as had been the case earlier in the battle. Continued aircraft losses at these levels left a serious deficit that could not be made up by the pace of deliveries from factories and repair depots.

Over this same period, Fighter Command had lost 97 pilots, with only 65 replacements coming out of the training schools. While this rang serious alarm bells at Bentley Priory, the more critical importance of this was that those lost had increasingly been combat veterans with experience from the initial phases of the battle. Progressively, it was the loss of these experienced pilots that was becoming the crucial factor. Replacement pilots were generally both inexperienced and insufficient in numbers to maintain the fighter units at their earlier effective strengths.

In an effort to accelerate the process of turning out combat-ready fighter pilots, training had already been cut from 44 weeks basic plus six weeks final training at OTUs to 22 weeks basic plus two weeks final training. In cases where the basic period showed a candidate to be exceptional, he was sometimes posted directly into squadron service. This understandably placed a heavy burden on the surviving, experienced RAF pilots, since they needed to lead as well as train the inexperienced newcomers, at the same time performing more operational sorties.

Constant fatigue was to become the norm during this critical time, as recalled by the likes of Bob Doe (Wing Commander R.F.T. Doe, DSO DFC) in recent television coverage of the battle. When his squadron was sent for a rest to the West Country, he recalled spending most of his first week away from the southeast sleeping. Elsewhere, one Spitfire ground crew, after seeing their aircraft land and taxi towards its blast pen, was perplexed and anxious when the machine rolled to a stop with its engine still turning over and no sign of the pilot emerging from the cockpit. Approaching the aircraft, they expected to find the pilot either dead at the controls, or badly wounded. Instead, he had simply fallen asleep, completely exhausted, not an uncommon experience over this period.

As casualties were replaced by less-experienced newcomers, British fighter losses also increased alarmingly. Replacement squadrons, used to quieter operational areas outside No. 11 Group, arrived in the hectic combat environment of the southeast unprepared for its stark reality. Most of them were blissfully unaware of how vulnerable regulation RAF formation tactics had already been shown to be, and how inappropriate to battle conditions their training in Fighting Area Attacks had become. Frequently, these squadrons experienced heavy losses in their early exposure to the skies over the Home Counties, many of them victims of the classic *Jagdwaffe* "bounce" that had come as such an unwelcome surprise to most No. 11 Group squadrons earlier in the battle. Everyone had to adapt or suffer. Some squadrons, newly arrived to No. 11 Group, suffering heavy casualties in the first few days of operations in the south, were rapidly moved back to quieter areas of operations to allow them to recover.

Polish pilots from 303 Squadron against a backdrop of one of the squadron's Hurricanes with the unit emblem just visible beneath the aircraft's radio antenna.

There were some noteworthy exceptions to this pattern of inexperienced squadron losses over this period. At the beginning of September, a number of squadrons were made operational with experienced fighter pilots who had fled from their European homelands as the German forces invaded them from the autumn of 1939. The nationalities of many countries were involved in this, Czechoslovakia, Poland, Belgium, Holland and France, all making important contributions.

None were more successful than the Polish squadrons, particularly 303 Squadron that was based at Northolt for much of the Battle of Britain. Viewed by the Air Ministry as potentially demoralised by the loss of their homeland, the Polish squadrons were considered to be of marginal value before they became operational. Even some of their British commanders, hampered by language difficulties and differences in temperament and upbringing, felt that the Polish fliers were not suited to the RAF style of flying and fighting. Many of the Poles however had already fought against the *Luftwaffe*, albeit briefly as their country was overrun, and they understood better than many of their RAF commanders how unsuited the RAF fighting tactics were in combat against the Germans.

When they were finally made operational, 303 Squadron soon demonstrated that their grasp of tactics and their flying skills were more than enough to ensure that they soon became the most successful fighter squadron during the Battle of Britain. Their record of victories over this period was never bettered, with the communal hatred of the Germans that had invaded their homeland a fundamental factor in this.

As the conflict entered the last week of August, metropolitan London experienced its first night attack by the bombers of the *Luftwaffe*. One of the raiders on the night of the 24th of August lost his bearings during a raid on Rochester and Thameshaven and mistakenly unloaded his bombs on the East End of London. Up until this time, Hitler had continued with his policy of leaving the capital unmolested, so this was effectively London's first experience of either night or day bombing. The damage to the south London outskirts of Croydon airport during the 15th of August was more clearly an unfortunate example of collateral damage, rather than a planned widening of the target area.

RAF Bomber Command retaliated to the London raid with its own night raids on Berlin from the 25th/26th of August. Even though these caused little real damage, it was sufficient to enrage Hitler, who became more receptive to the argument of both Goering and Kesserling that lifting his earlier restriction on attacks against London was now the way to persuade Britain to seek peace terms.

This change of direction signalled the beginning of the next phase of the battle - the continuous bombing of London. Disastrous and terrifying though this was for the London population, it was to give much needed relief for No. 11 Group's squadrons, as well as allowing Fighter Command to repair damage to the detection and control links that were so critical to the whole air defence mechanism in the southeast.

<u>Local Casualties 24th August - 6th September 1940</u>

5.   <u>Bf 109 E-4 of JG 3 crash-landed on 29th August near Pevensey</u>

The 29th of August turned out to be one of the last days of the summer months when weather conditions in the Channel area limited offensive action by the *Luftwaffe* throughout the day. It was not until 1445 hours that the south of England's radar stations began to identify the build-up of a large German formation heading for the Sussex coast at Beachy Head. It soon became clear that the approaching force was made up mainly of fighters, some 500 Bf 109s from JG 3, JG 26 and JG 51, together with 150 Bf 110s from ZG 26 and ZG 76, all escorting a small formation of *Heinkel* He 111s and *Dornier* Do 17s.

Generalfeldmarschall Albert Kesserling, the commander of *Luftflotte* 2, had by this time formulated his own mix of tactics, aimed at giving his recently-appointed *Jagdwaffe* leaders the best chance of knocking out more of Fighter Command's aircraft. By sending a few bombers, escorted by such a mass of fighters, he knew it would be difficult for No. 11 Group to ignore this attack. He anticipated that when the Spitfires and Hurricanes rose to intercept the German formation, they would be swamped by the German fighters, suffering the sort of high casualty rates that he knew were required to prepare for the invasion, still then scheduled for mid-September.

Although as many as 13 squadrons from No. 11 group were scrambled to meet the German force, many of these were recalled when it became obvious that the number of bombers in the formation was comparatively small. Dowding's priority remained keeping fighter reserves to break up the larger bomber formations when they appeared. This demanded that such an attacking formation, mainly made up of fighters, should either be ignored or countered by limited forces.

Despite this, Hurricanes of 85 Squadron (Croydon) together with Spitfires of 603 Squadron (Hornchurch) and 610 Squadron (Biggin Hill) attacked the German formations along the Sussex coast around Eastbourne and Hastings, and a number of Bf 109s were damaged or destroyed. Among these was "Black 8" of the 2nd *Staffel* JG 3, piloted by *Oberfeldwebel* (Flight Sergeant) Bernhard Lempskemper. He force-landed close to the Chain Home RDF station, near Newhouse Farm, Church Acre, on the Pevensey Marshes outside Eastbourne.

For both British and German aircraft, damaged or running low on fuel, the flat, marshy fields to the northeast of Eastbourne between Hankham and Hurstmonceux must have offered a welcome and comparatively dry alternative to the inhospitable waters of the Channel, despite the inherent dangers of the radar pylons, electricity transmission lines, and the local air defences around the radar site.

Messerschmitt Bf 109s from Lempskemper's 2nd Staffel JG 3 are prepared for a sortie from an airfield in northern France, with ground crew completing final preparations before take-off.

Lempskemper had crossed the English coast at 22,000 ft slightly ahead of the other members of the 2nd *Staffel* when he was attacked by some of the defending fighters. His aircraft loss is attributed to Sergeant Glendon Bulmar Booth in a Hurricane of Green Section, 85 Squadron. Lempskemper was another *Luftwaffe* pilot who seemed to suffer from "Spitfire snobbery", since his interrogation shows that he thought he'd been attacked by Spitfires rather than Hurricanes.

As he was attacked, the German pilot's engine seized, but he eventually succeeded in making a smooth force-landing at 1525 hours. Approaching the ground at only 300 feet on a dead engine, he was targeted by some of the Bofors gun anti aircraft crews around the sensitive Pevensey radar site. Their fire caused extensive damage to the aircraft's undersides and Lempskemper eventually joined the growing ranks of *Luftwaffe* aircrew destined for POW camps, both in the British Isles and Canada.

20-year old Sergeant Booth's combat report on the 29th of August claimed a Bf 109 as a probable kill at 1600 hours during combat over the Hastings area.

As Green 2, I was below the main mass of enemy aircraft when I saw five Me 109s in front and to the right of myself. These aircraft were not in formation. I attached myself to the tail of one and gave a short burst at about 100 yards range from astern. The Me 109 dived and was emitting thick black smoke. I followed the aircraft down and continued firing in bursts. I continued the chase till about 10 miles out to sea off Eastbourne. We were then about 500 ft high. The enemy aircraft was still losing height and giving out black smoke when I left it.

Sergeant Booth's Hurricane (P2879) was badly damaged later that afternoon, eventually landing back at Croydon for repair with the pilot unhurt. He was not so lucky four days later, on the 1st of September 1940. He baled out of his burning Hurricane (VY-O with registration L2071) too late to prevent damage to his parachute. Descending below only a partially effective parachute, he crashed to earth breaking his back and limbs. Despite being admitted to Purley Hospital, he died of his injuries on the 7th of February 1941. Although he died five months later, he effectively became one of three of 85 Squadron's pilots to perish during that early September action over Kent and Surrey. Four other 85 Squadron aircraft were also damaged at that time, some with pilots wounded.

6.   Bf 109 E-1 of JG 3 crashed on 29th August near Hooe

Only one RAF fighter pilot was killed during the early afternoon engagements against the attacking German forces on the 29th of August, this being a pilot from 610 Squadron based at Biggin Hill. Despite this, several others were wounded or baled out of their damaged aircraft. By the end of the day, after a second wave of attacks in the early evening, a second RAF pilot was killed, this time one of Sergeant Booth's colleagues from 85 Squadron.

By contrast, casualties from the German fighter units on the 29th of August were much higher, with nine Bf 109s destroyed and seven of the pilots either killed, missing or prisoners of war. This pattern of casualties among the *Jagdwaffe* fighters was becoming a more regular feature of the massed air battles over the southeast. This highlighted that trying to destroy Fighter Command by swamping them with huge numbers of German fighter escorts was as likely to cause casualties in the *Luftwaffe*, as it was among the British squadrons. In many instances, as the British fighters returned to base to rearm and refuel, with other British units carrying on the battles, there were frequently more German targets than British, with the predictable result that it was the *Jagdwaffe* that suffered. This became a typical outcome of the growing intensity of the attacks towards the end of August and early September, following Goering's demands for his fighters to be more aggressive.

The second major attack on the 29th of August came around 1830 hours, when another massed formation of German fighters was sent from their bases in northern France to tempt British fighters into action. Three British squadrons were sent to counter clouds of Bf 109s and Bf 110s, with Hurricanes from 85 and 501 Squadrons and Spitfires from 603 Squadron again benefitting from the target-rich environment. This time, the bulk of the action occurred further along the coast, east of the Kent/Sussex borders, and most of the British aircraft casualties fell between Hawkinge and Rye.

Many of the *Luftwaffe* casualties fell in the Channel, with some of the pilots rescued by the German *Seenotflug Kommando* air-sea rescue planes. Others were simply posted as missing, not an uncommon end for many *Jagdwaffe* pilots as they struggled to nurse their aircraft back to France, sometimes damaged, but always low on fuel.

JG 3 was once more in the midst of this action, and aircraft from the 4th *Staffel* were involved in combat further west than the main force. Two Bf 109s from this unit were shot down in action over Hastings, with one crashing to destruction at 1900 hours on the fields of New Lodge Farm, Hooe. This was the Bf 109 E-1 piloted by *Oberleutnant* Jost Kipper, who died when his parachute failed to open. Reports at the time pointed to his family name being Wipper but he is shown as Jost Kipper at the German War Graves Commission cemetery at Cannock Chase, where the body of the pilot was finally interred.

The headstone in memory of Oberleutnant Jost Kipper, now buried at the German War Graves Commission cemetery at Cannock Chase along with two other Luftwaffe airmen who died during World War Two.

JG 3, involved in both of the afternoon sorties on the 29th of August, was badly mauled. They finished the day losing six Bf 109s with a further two aircraft damaged. In all, the *Luftwaffe* lost 24 aircraft and 45 crew members, with Fighter Command losing ten aircraft and one pilot. The German fighter losses in all totalled nine Bf 109s destroyed, with an additional four of these increasingly-crucial interceptors damaged. As far as fighter : fighter losses were concerned, neither side had achieved a resounding success, but the pilot and Bf 109 losses were becoming increasingly telling for the *Jagdwaffe*.

The results of the day underlined that where large formations met and engaged, the confusion of the engagements often left neither side with much advantage. In all probability, the pilots on both sides spent more time frantically trying to avoid colliding and taking snap shots at passing targets than actually stalking victims.

Albert Kesserling's plan to swamp Fighter Command with overwhelming German fighter superiority and impose heavy losses on the defending British squadrons was a resounding failure on the 29th of August.

Another group of JG 3 Messerschmitt Bf 109s, probably from the 3rd Staffel, wait for their pilots' next mission as their ground crews make final preparations for the mission.

Carefully evaluated interceptions by limited RAF fighter numbers conserved the fighter reserves as much as possible to hit the bombers when they came. This limited Fighter Command reaction to German fighter sorties also minimised the growing problem of pilot availability and, in particular, the rapidly dwindling ranks of combat-experienced flight and squadron leaders.

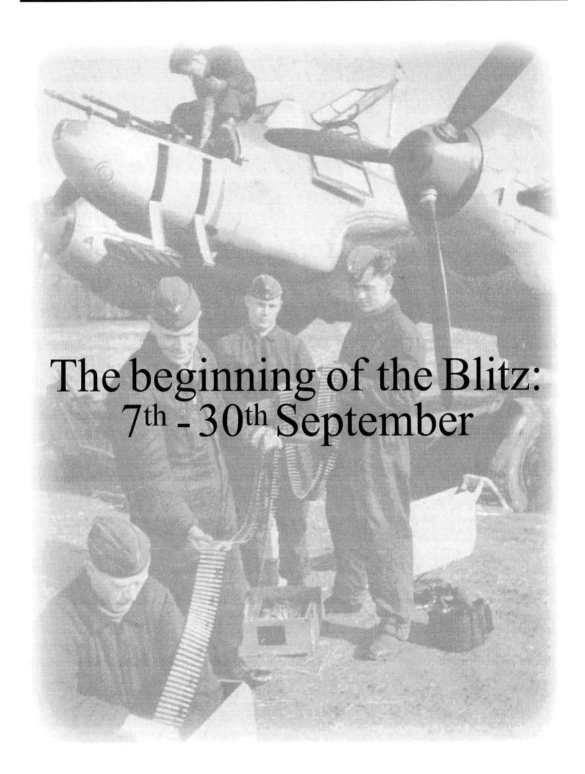

The beginning of the Blitz:
7th - 30th September

The beginning of the Blitz : 7th - 30th September

As August passed and September began, both Dowding and Park recognised that a few more days of the heavy attacks that were being made on No. 11 Group's airfields would make modified tactics necessary if the Group was to retain its function as a cohesive force.

A pivotal meeting was held on the 7th of September between Dowding, accompanied by his colleagues in No. 11 Group, and the Air Ministry. The purpose of the meeting was to evaluate the best methods of maintaining an effective defence of the southeast, taking into account the pilot attrition that had been suffered. Up till the end of August, losses of Spitfire and Hurricane pilots had totalled 348, while the training system had produced 280 qualified pilots since the beginning of the battles. Whatever the level of aircraft production, if pilot losses at these levels continued and the German offensive remained at a constant level, the effectiveness of the southeast's air defences was under severe threat.

Disguised by the neutrality of statistics was the inevitable fact that the RAF losses had been mainly experienced pilots and unit commanders, many of whom had been in action since before the fall of France. The replacements, by necessity mostly fresh from training schools, conversion courses from other RAF commands, and generally with little experience of the thoroughbred monoplane fighters that they were to fly, were ill suited to fill the gaps left by the August losses. The training units had already been called upon to curtail training periods drastically and leave "the final polish" to operational combat flying.

If the focus of the mass attacks by the *Luftwaffe* had remained fixed on the southeast's airfields, many found it difficult to imagine that No. 11 Group could maintain its effectiveness much beyond the first ten days of September. The temptation to withdraw many of No. 11 Group's squadrons to bases further north and west must have increased to the point where the potential loss of morale this may have caused, both in the services and the general population, may have been considered a necessary sacrifice.

Hitler's reaction to Bomber Command's night time bombing of Berlin towards the end of August was the pivotal element that changed the fortunes of RAF Fighter Command at this point. At a meeting in the Hague on the 3rd of September, Goering had been persuaded by *Generalfeldmarschall* Albert Kesserling - the commander of *Luftflotte* 2 - to concentrate attacks on London, rather than continuing the assault against Fighter Command. He was vehemently opposed by *Generalfeldmarschall* Hugo Sperrle - the commander of *Luftflotte* 3, who was known to take some pleasure from arguing with Kesserling. Sperrle advocated continuing the bombing attacks on Fighter Command airfields as the only logical way to ensure German control of the British airspace that was critical to any invasion plans.

Goering had already decided that Hitler was unlikely to go ahead with the invasion of Britain. Perhaps seeing his favoured position with Hitler eroded by the damage that ever-present Hurricanes and Spitfires of Fighter Command were wreaking on the *Luftwaffe*, he knew he had to be seen to be decisive in his efforts to make good his earlier boasts to Hitler. He had grown used to the trappings of power that had followed his rise in the Nazi party and the early successes of the *Luftwaffe*.

With the assault on the airfields apparently having little effect on the numbers of British fighters rising to meet the German raids, he decided to persuade Hitler that now was the time to bomb London. Angered by the British raids on Berlin, Hitler was not difficult to persuade and, on the 4th of September, he theatrically announced his decision to throw the full weight of the *Luftwaffe* against London in front of a largely female audience at Berlin's *Sportpalast*.

In the aftermath of the continuous attacks on No. 11 Group's airfields through the end of August and early September, the controllers and tracking rooms waited with trepidation for the first of the attacks on the 7th of September. Unaware of the change in German tactics, the fear throughout Fighter Command was that the day would bring more heavy bombing sorties against British airfields at a time when the fighter squadrons were struggling to recover from the damage and losses of the previous few days.

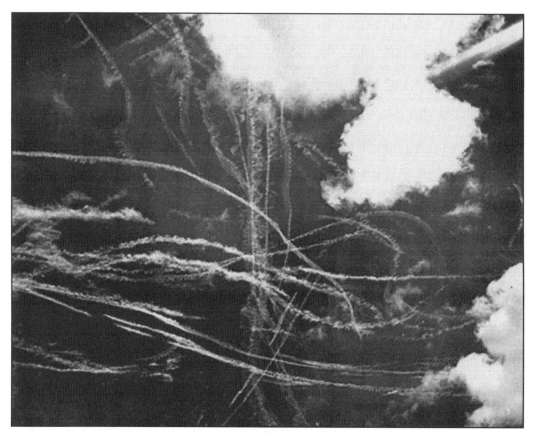

High over the countryside of southern England, a complicated web of vapour trails identify the battles going on overhead between British fighters and the Luftwaffe bombers and fighters during late summer 1940. (Kent Messenger Newspaper Group)

The day opened with the weather promising a repetition of the preceding few days, sunny, hot and comparatively cloudless. The morning passed with negligible activity, but by 1600 hours the radar operators began to see a huge build up of German aircraft over the French coast. This was gradually identified as some 300 medium bombers, with an escort of 600 Bf 109 and 200 Bf 110 fighters. Anticipating continued attacks on the southeast's airfields and other strategic targets such as the Thameshaven oil refinery, four squadrons were scrambled to take up positions to defend these targets. When the attacking *Luftwaffe* armada reached the point where it would normally break into individual groups aiming for separate targets, the whole force droned resolutely towards the capital.

Over the next hour, a further 18 squadrons were scrambled to meet the masses of approaching German aircraft, as it became clear that London was the target. Despite the numbers of RAF fighters involved and the intensity of their attacks on the bomber formations, the sheer scale of the German attack allowed many of the bombers to unload their bombs over the capital, and London began to suffer its first saturation bombing. Part of the reason for this was the relatively late realisation that the target focus had switched to London rather than the airfields. This meant that comparatively few of the intercepting RAF fighters managed to reach the bomber formations before their bomb loads had been released and the bombers were on their way back to home base.

Forming a backdrop to the image of Tower Bridge and the Tower of London, the capital's docklands burn after the attacks by the Luftwaffe began on 7 September 1940.

These sorties continued after dark, with the last German bombers not leaving until 0430 hours the following morning. Although by the end of the month the *Luftwaffe* had learned to its cost that daylight attacks on Britain's capital were too dangerous to continue in the face of increasingly aggressive response from RAF fighters, the night sorties continued for 57 consecutive nights. For the German bombers on subsequent night raids on London, any problems of target identification were solved simply by aiming at the smoke and flames from the previous raids.

Despite the horrific experiences of the London population over this period, this target switch allowed RAF Fighter Command to regain its strength and continue to punish the German daylight raids until the end of September, when the *Luftwaffe* recognised such mass raids were costing too many men and machines.

Throughout all of this, the background thought in the minds of most of both British and German high commands was that these raids were either the preparation for the forthcoming invasion, or alternatively to bring public pressure on the British government to sue for peace. Hitler had scheduled Operation Sea Lion for the middle of September, a target date that was increasingly at risk from both the continued strength demonstrated by the RAF fighters, and the inevitability of less benevolent weather as autumn took its hold.

Between the 7th and the 15th of September 1940, daylight activities by the *Luftwaffe* slackened off as weather conditions again deteriorated, allowing Dowding to implement the plans he had proposed to the Air Ministry during the meeting held on the 7th of September.

The beginning of the Blitz : 7th - 30th September

These plans focussed on maintaining as close as possible to full strength the squadrons operating within the pivotal No. 11 Group area - category "A" squadrons. These included those units from No. 10 and No. 12 Groups that were frequently called to support the threatened southeast sector. Category "B" squadrons were generally experienced units based outside No. 11 Group. They were maintained as close as possible to full strength in order to provide a reserve to be called into the southeast as replacements for tired or depleted squadrons when necessary. Category "C" units were those based in more remote areas of Britain, for whom losses, exhaustion or training levels made it inadvisable to commit them to the battles over the southeast. These units were progressively used as the basis for training, providing the intermediate stage between the training schools and front line squadrons operating in the intensive combat areas of the southeast.

The period up until the middle of September saw the *Luftwaffe* building up for a major onslaught, throwing enormous fighter and bomber strength into an apparently all-out effort to force Britain into submission by mass attacks on London and its suburbs on the 15th of September. Smaller raids were also conducted on Portland and Southampton.

Remembered today as "Battle of Britain Day", the 15th of September 1940 saw the heaviest losses of men and aircrew on both sides throughout the whole period of the battle. Even though the German casualties on both the 15th and 18th of August, one month earlier, were higher than the 93 airmen and 61 aircraft that were lost on the 15th of September, RAF losses of 16 airmen and 31 aircraft were close to the highest of any single day through the four month battle. The 15th, 27th and 30th days of September effectively became the last days when the *Luftwaffe* risked such large-scale daylight bombing formations.

Such was the impact of the defence put up by Fighter Command on the 15th of September that Operation Sea Lion, already rescheduled for the 21st of the month, was postponed indefinitely. It had finally become clear to German High Command that they would be unable to achieve the air supremacy that they needed to allow any invasion to force and hold a successful beachhead on the English south coast during 1940.

On the 17th of September, various signals were intercepted by the British intelligence groups listening to German radio traffic, all of which signalled the deferment of the invasion. Paradoxically, it was not until much later in the war that the plan for an invasion of Britain was officially cancelled by German High Command. Following the autumn of 1940, the threat of an invasion of Britain was seen as an important element in maintaining psychological pressure on Britain. Grand Admiral Erich Raeder's entry in the official German War Diary for the 17th of September included the observation:

> *The enemy air force is by no means defeated. On the contrary, it shows increasing activity.........The Fuehrer decides to postpone Operation Sealion indefinitely.*

During the next eight months, Hitler made his preparations for the invasion of the Balkans and Greece, followed by Operation Barbarossa, the attack on Russia which finally started in June 1941. With the *Luftwaffe* seriously depleted of aircraft, and more importantly, experienced leaders and other aircrew by the losses suffered during the Battle of Britain, this operation ultimately proved one step too many.

Recent computer analysis of the Battle of Britain has raised some interesting questions over the importance of the *Luftwaffe's* switch of targets to concentrate on London. Historically, this is seen as fundamental to Fighter Command's survival over that period. The generally-held view is that, had the German raids on No. 11 Group's airfields continued through September, the squadrons based in the southeast would, at the very least, have been forced to withdraw further into the centre of the country, potentially leaving the south coast more open to any planned invasion.

This computer analysis takes a different view. Had the German tactics not changed in early September, and both sides continued to suffer loss rates over the autumn similar to those experienced during July and August, this study points towards the *Luftwaffe* soon reaching untenable operational strength, while RAF strength would have stayed relatively constant. Pivotally, Germany was not equipped to fight a prolonged war against an effective adversary that was able to withstand such a sustained conflict.

Thanks to Lord Beaverbrook controlling British aircraft production, replacement aircraft were continuing to reach front line squadrons in numbers that were more than sufficient to replace the losses most of the time, apart from during some of August. Undoubtedly, experienced pilot losses remained a more critical factor, with fresh replacements unable to fill the gaps adequately.

An engineer works on the engine bay of a Spitfire at the Castle Bromwich factory set up as part of Lord Beaverbrook's efforts to boost aircraft production.

However, on the German side, the situation was worse. Pilot, aircrew and aircraft losses were becoming even more damaging than they were for Fighter Command. Ignoring for the moment the disparity in aircraft crew numbers between fighters and bombers, the problem for the *Luftwaffe* was that they spent the bulk of their operational sorties over England and the Channel. Aircraft lost over England meant crew personnel either killed or captured, but in either case the demand for trained replacements increased.

Many aircraft ditched in the inhospitable Channel, and while various crew members were recovered by the German rescue services, the majority still remain listed as "missing" even today, victims of cold, exhaustion and drowning. The effect of this on *Luftwaffe* operational strength is easy to see.

Despite German rescue services being better organised than the rather haphazard arrangements that the British had put in place up until this point, the odds against rescue of any aircrew in the Channel were always in the sea's favour. For ditched *Luftwaffe* pilots, it was not unknown for some, despairing of rescue, to choose to end their own suffering with a bullet from their service pistols, rather than endure a lingering death from exposure and drowning. *Jagdwaffe* pilots were eventually forbidden to take their service pistols on missions against England in an effort to minimise the demoralising effect of dead pilot's bodies being washed up from the sea with a single bullet hole in the head.

In contrast to the *Luftwaffe* experience, British pilots were generally operating over the Home Counties where there was always the possibility of a successful crash-landing or, if they baled out, a good chance that they may be back in action the same day. Even for RAF pilots who chased fleeing German aircraft over the Channel, there was still a reasonable chance of struggling back to the British coast, even on a dead engine or out of fuel. These options were not always without fatal mishaps, but served to give Fighter Command a better chance of recovering pilots than was the case for the *Luftwaffe*.

Production of the Bf 109 fighter, still the only weapon in the *Luftwaffe* armoury capable of taking on the British fighters on equal terms, rarely exceeded the attrition rates of the May/September 1940 period. Monthly production of this fighter in 1940 fluctuated enormously over the summer months, with output at two of the plants being limited to a six hour day, instead of the 10-12 hour days that were really required. When pressed by one of his subordinates to order the aircraft plants to boost production, Goering treated the request with joking disdain, apparently choosing to ignore the full impact of the losses his fighters were suffering. Roughly 700 Bf 109s were delivered from the factories over May/September 1940. During this same period, a similar number of single engine fighters were lost either in combat or through domestic accident. The other main aircraft types flown by the *Luftwaffe* (heavy fighters, bombers and dive-bombers) were being manufactured over this period in numbers that exceeded the losses incurred by some margin, although it was close for the bombers - 1,142 losses against 1,160 replacements.

During the early part of the World War Two, there had been little concerted effort to co-ordinate and maximise German armaments' production to deal with the requirements of a prolonged war situation. The early successes in Europe, combined with Hitler's expectation that Britain would soon come to terms, were all factors that prevented German industry from being allocated the co-ordinated financial and material support needed to reach a more organised war footing.

Compared to the impact this had on the German Army and Navy, for the *Luftwaffe*, the effect of this was worse. As the newest arm of the German Armed Forces, it had been expanded at such a rate from its inception in 1934 that there was little unified control over almost every part of its structure. Much against the accepted view of the German character, inefficiency was also rife among the aircraft producers. Senior figures involved in planning and supply were also constantly manoeuvring for personal advancement or following a personal agenda. While some of these had experience of wartime flying from World War One, a number of these were Goering's friends from that conflict. Some, like Ernst Udet, were exceptional flyers but, like Goering himself, unsuited to management and planning. Many others came from other branches of the Armed Forces and had no technical knowledge of either aircraft or aerial tactics. It was not until much later in the war, after the retreat from Russia, that the armaments' industry was stimulated to new heights of ingenuity and production, ultimately in the defence of Germany from both Russia and the western allies.

If the mass bombing raids on the southeast of Britain had continued on the scale seen in August and early September, with the bombers requiring the saturation direct and indirect escorts of Bf 109s that had become standard, then the *Luftwaffe* would have progressively lost more of its fighters, leaving fewer and fewer escort units for subsequent missions. It was not uncommon over this period for the fighter : bomber ratio of German daylight raids to be three or more fighters for each bomber attacking London and the southeast.

There is therefore a convincing case for the argument that, with British aircraft replacement levels remaining relatively constant, this would ultimately have degraded the *Luftwaffe* escort capability sufficiently to undermine the viability of continued attacks on Britain on the massive scale seen during much of August and September.

The target focus for the *Luftwaffe* nevertheless did change, and whatever the outcome might have been had the targets remained the airfields, the result for tired RAF fighter squadrons was a temporary reprieve that allowed them time to recover from the damage of the previous month, as it also did for Fighter Command's communications and control infrastructure.

As the mass bombing raids developed from the second half of August onwards, important tactical changes had been made in the way the *Luftwaffe's* Bf 109 fighters were employed. Goering's bomber commanders had continued to blame their mounting losses on the lack of adequate close protection from the fighters. These still favoured operating at least 10,000 feet above the operational height of most of the bomber formations, from where they could dive to attack the RAF units as they came to intercept the bombers. The bomber crews, faced with the knowledge that it was they, rather than the fighters, that were the targets for Fighter Command, needed both the physical protection and the psychological comfort of seeing their German fighter units in close proximity to their own formations.

The bomber commanders argued that the *Jagdwaffe* preference to base their defensive strategy for the bombers on their normal "bounce" tactics, often left the bomber formations temporarily unprotected against climbing British fighters. Normally, once the British fighters had been spotted, the leader of the German fighters would manoeuvre his unit at high altitude into a favourable position to attack out of the sun, before diving to the attack. These manoeuvres of course took time, sometimes too much time to prevent the British fighters launching unopposed attacks on the comparatively helpless bombers. Having suffered losses in this way, it was unsurprising that the bomber crews felt abandoned and unprotected, and that they made their feelings abundantly clear to Goering and his staff.

In an effort to create a fighter force that could perform the role of both high cover and close escort, Goering had earlier transferred control of almost all the single engine fighters from *Luftflotte* 3 (western France) to *Luftflotte* 2 in the Calais area, where their limited range would offer the least handicap. JG 2 (Richthofen) was the only fighter group to remain at their bases near the Normandy coast. These transfers had been put into effect between the 19th and the 24th of August and by early September, they were fully integrated into a strike force immediately across the Channel from Dover.

The nose section of the Heinkel He 111, showing how vulnerable to frontal attack these aircraft were. Even the pilot, sitting at the rear of the cabin protected to the rear by armour plate was at risk from a frontal attack.

With the fighter numbers available for escort duty swollen in this way, Goering insisted that a proportion of fighter escorts should abandon their traditional top cover position, and fly close escort at the same altitude as the bombers. It was left to the individual commanders of the *Jagdwaffe* units to decide how this was to be translated into operational practice. JG 26 for instance, arguably one of the more successful fighter units, chose to use its individual units in different patterns. Some *staffeln* would range ahead of the main bomber force in the usual high altitude, *freie Jagd,* sorties to try to lure the British fighters into the air early. The bombers would have others close by as direct escort, with still more slightly higher as indirect escort. Behind the bomber formations, yet further German fighters would operate as high-level escort, protecting the formation from attack from the rear. A rearguard force would remain on the ground in France until they could rendezvous with the returning bomber stream and replace the German fighters which would have already been returning to France low on fuel.

The effects of limiting the number of Bf 109s operating as top cover were telling. In practical terms, it brought a proportion of the fighter cover down to the bombers' normal height of 15,000 - 18,000 feet. This took away the all-important advantage of height that the German fighters had normally established as they gathered over the French coast and crossed the Channel.

With significantly lower wing loadings than the Bf 109, both the Hurricane and Spitfire were more agile below 20,000 feet, but they took almost 15 minutes to climb to 25,000 feet, with the Hurricane becoming particularly sluggish as it gained height. In the early days of the conflict, the advantage of height had allowed the Bf 109s to employ the "bounce" techniques of attack on the climbing, sometimes unaware, British fighters. Operating as close escort took this away, simultaneously increasing German fighter losses, a development that in reality they could ill afford.

The German pilots operating as close escort lost their ability to choose the time and position of attack, since they were constrained by the timing of the RAF attacks on the bombers. The mental strain of this on the German pilots was multiplied since the close escort Bf 109s regularly had to weave or fly with flaps down in order to maintain formation with the slower bombers. These manoeuvres caused extra fatigue and used up already-precious fuel reserves.

The *Heinkel* He 111 medium bomber had a maximum loaded speed of about 200 mph, while both the Bf 109 and Bf 110 had maximum speeds of around 350 mph and cruising speeds around 300 mph. Even the faster *Junkers* Ju 88, whose maximum unloaded speed was almost 290 mph, cruised in loaded configuration at less than 250 mph, and the slower He 111 and *Dornier* Do 17 bombers were by far the most widely used during the early part of the Battle of Britain. In practical terms, this meant that German bomber formations approached their targets in Southern England at little more than 160 mph, denying most of the close escort fighters the two elements that fighter pilots value above all else - superior height and speed.

As the German fighter pilots were inevitably forced to engage in furious dogfights with the British Hurricanes and Spitfires, further problems were created. The Bf 110 became especially vulnerable in this sort of role, and the onus fell more and more on the single engine Bf 109 to defend both the bombers and ironically the heavy fighters against the more nimble British aircraft.

The *Zerstoerer* units continued to make up the fighter numbers on many of the sorties, in particular against London right up until the end of September. This was not solely due to the fuel limitations of the Bf 109 but because progressively there weren't enough Bf 109s to produce the fighter escort ratio demanded by the bomber groups. Escort duty for bombing sorties that continued against British airfields north of the Thames (North Weald, Hornchurch, Debden and particularly Duxford) had to be left to the heavy fighters simply because the Bf 109 did not have sufficient range to continue far beyond London. The Bf 110 casualties on these missions were understandably very heavy.

Eventually, their losses reached levels that caused *OKL* to withdraw most of the Bf 110 units from the Channel front. Many of these were transferred to night fighter duties in the defence of Germany against British bomber attacks. When Hitler finally launched his offensive against Russia later in 1941, Bf 110 units were allocated to that theatre, where they were particularly effective in the close support fighter-bomber role, as well as operating in the Mediterranean and North African campaigns.

As September passed, the German fighters suffered increasing losses as many of them were necessarily obliged to surrender the height advantage that had served them so well up until this time. During September, as bomber casualties fell off marginally, fighters rarely represented less than half of the German losses as the demand for close escorts rose. The majority of these were Bf 109s, forced increasingly to replace the dwindling ranks of the *Zerstoerer* units in the role of close bomber escort.

Much has been made, and rightly so, of the exhaustion and dangers for the RAF pilots as air battles continued at a hectic pace. However, the German pilots were also suffering badly. They still operated almost entirely over hostile territory, as well as over the inhospitable waters of the Channel, which remained the heavy psychological burden for most pilots every time they listened to another operational briefing. For all the Bf 109 pilots flying over southern Britain, one of the most important disciplines, other than avoiding being shot down, was a constant check on fuel status to ensure there was sufficient fuel to get home to France. This became an essential pre-occupation that was made more frustrating when the fighter units had to waste fuel waiting to rendezvous with the bombers.

RAF Fighter Command was in a position to rotate tired and depleted squadrons away from the hectic southeast to other parts of the country where they could recuperate, bringing in fresh or rested squadrons from those more remote areas. The German units had no such luxury. Most of them stayed on active duty from May 1940 throughout the Battle of Britain, there being little in the way of reserve units to give battle-weary squadrons the opportunity for rest.

From the limited perspective of local casualties, any change in the ratio of bomber : fighter casualties was not readily apparent, since the only *Luftwaffe* medium bombers that came to earth in

The beginning of the Blitz : 7th - 30th September

Sussex during the Battle of Britain period fell outside the local Eastbourne area. Apart from some bombers that came down in the sea and therefore were less visible examples of the damage the RAF fighters were wreaking, the closest to this part of Sussex were near Battle and Blackboys. All of the casualties that fell around Eastbourne over this period, both British and German, were single or twin-engine fighters or fighter-bombers.

Showing signs of souvenir hunters and recovery of useful machinery by RAF intelligence, this Junkers Ju88 from Stab KG 30 was brought down on 9 September 1940. It crash-landed at Church Field, Newells Farm, near Horsham. (MB)

As one of the most prominent landmarks from the air on the south coast, Beachy Head and the area inland around Eastbourne bore witness to the intensity of the air war during this part of September. It was a similar story over much of the south as summer came to a close and autumn began.

Local Casualties 7th - 30th September

7. Hurricane 1 of 607 Squadron crashed on 9th September at Pevensey

After the surprise change of targets for the German bomber formations on the 7th of September, Fighter Command was better prepared to meet the attacks on London over the next few days. The *Luftwaffe* formations followed similar approach paths to their targets in the London area as they had on the 7th of September, with the result that the RAF controllers were better prepared to position squadrons to meet these attacks. Both on the 8th and 9th of September, fewer bombers actually reached their target areas in the capital compared to the events of the first London raids, most turning back in the face of heavy resistance from the RAF fighters. In these later attacks, the incoming raiders were also hampered by strong headwinds, which gave the defending fighters extra time and speed to gain the advantage of both height and position.

The 9th of September began with less than perfect weather conditions, with scattered showers and the risk of thunderstorms. However, by 1700 hours, following an advance guard of high-flying Bf 109s, the bombers were again detected en route towards London. Some 300 German aircraft made up the attacking formation, *Heinkel* He 111, *Junkers* Ju 88 and *Dornier* Do 17 bombers, with a close escort of both Bf 109 and Bf 110 fighters. As many as 14 squadrons of Hurricanes and Spitfires were sent against the German bombers, making numerous interceptions during the next hour stretching from the Kent and Sussex coasts to the London outskirts. By the end of the day, the RAF had lost 25 aircraft destroyed with the loss of 16 pilots, but the German losses totalled 41 aircraft and 52 aircrew.

One of the British squadrons in action over the Mayfield area during the late afternoon was 607 Squadron, flying Hurricanes out of Tangmere. By the day's close, at least four of their Hurricanes were destroyed, with a further machine damaged but repairable. Even worse however, three of the pilots were killed and two others wounded. 607 Squadron had only moved to Tangmere on the 1st of September, having come down from Usworth in No. 13 Group area in the comparatively quiet northeast. They replaced 17 Squadron who moved to Debden in No. 10 Group after two weeks of hectic action.

The 13 aircraft from the squadron had been ordered to patrol the Mayfield area and around 1730 hours they attempted to intercept a formation of *Junkers* Ju 88 and *Heinkel* He 111 bombers that were moving steadily towards London in groups of five aircraft. Squadron Leader James Vick ordered 607 Squadron towards the bombers, but soon spotted Bf 109 escorts at 19,000 feet on both sides of the bomber formation, as well as trailing behind. Blue section was ordered to attack the bombers, while Green section remained as a rear guard against the escorting fighters. However, it soon became apparent that the bomber formation was too far ahead to be overhauled and attacked by 607 Squadron's Hurricanes. S/L Vick then ordered both Red and Yellow sections to attack the escorting German fighters.

607 Squadron was not new to action against the *Luftwaffe*, having been sent to France as part of the Air Component of the BEF before the fall of France. After Dunkirk, they had rested and re-equipped in the northeast of England, finally to be drafted back to the vicious fighting in the southeast that typified the end of August and the beginning of September 1940. Their earlier experiences in France should have prevented them from making the same mistake that many squadrons fresh to No. 11 Group made in the period immediately after their arrival there. Nevertheless, 607 Squadron finished the day chastened by the attacks of the bombers' escorting Bf 109s, probably from JG 27.

One of the squadron's Hurricanes was reported to have crashed at Squire's Field in Pevensey as a result of this action, with the pilot baling out. It's not been possible to clarify this at the time of writing. The squadron's Operations Record Book for the 9th of September 1940 shows the roster for this sortie during the late afternoon, as well as the casualties that evening, both killed and wounded.

The tally of casualties and the location of their aircraft crashes in fact do not support the concept that one of their aircraft came to earth in the Pevensey area as a result of this sortie. All of the aircraft from 607 squadron that are known to have crashed that evening finished up north of the Weald, on a line roughly from Goudhurst to just north of Sevenoaks, with their locations clear from either contemporary reports or more recent excavations. It's therefore difficult to believe that any Hurricane that crashed near Pevensey that evening was had been part of the 607 squadron roster.

At the time of writing, I can find nothing that would suggest a Hurricane from any other squadron was involved and no further details have become clear. Even the location of the crash remains a matter of some confusion.

8.   <u>Hurricane 1 of 238 Squadron force-landed on 13th September near Lower Dicker</u>

As the summer came to a close and the weather became increasingly unsettled, bombing sorties by the *Luftwaffe* continued to be scaled down, allowing most of No. 11 Group's fighter squadrons to regain some of the operational strength that had been lost since the middle of August. The deteriorating weather did not frustrate all German attacks, but without the clear and sunny conditions of high summer, missions were reduced in scale, and the bombers frequently aborted the raids against London targets in the face of both determined fighter defence from the RAF and cloud cover over their targets.

Hurricanes of 238 Squadron at dispersal.

The 13th of September was a wet, misty day with consistent cloud and rain, conditions that encouraged neither large-scale raids by the *Luftwaffe*, nor regular interceptions by Fighter Command. With more limited offensive activity, casualties were reduced on both sides, and the only local incident centred on the force-landing of a 238 Squadron Hurricane from Middle Wallop in No. 10 Group area.

The squadron had been sent to patrol the Tangmere/Hailsham sector in Sussex, and while patrolling this area at 10,000 feet, Green section spotted and chased a *Junkers* Ju 88, firing several bursts of fire at long range, without effect.

Canadian Pilot Officer John R. Urwin-Mann was involved in the interception but ran out of fuel. He made a force-landing near Perrylands Wood, north of Lower Dicker at 1655 hours. His aircraft sustained little damage during the landing and, after it was refuelled, he managed to fly back to Tangmere where he landed and spent the night before returning to Middle Wallop the next day.

9.   <u>Bf 109 E-1 of JG 27 crashed on 27th September near Selmeston</u>

The weather forecast for the 27th of September promised favourable conditions over the Channel and the southern part of Britain. High cloud ceiling at 25,000 ft was to provide a backdrop to intermittent cloud cover between 7,000 and 10,000 ft, with some light rain.

In the early morning, the pilots of some 40 Bf 109s from I. and II.*Gruppen* /JG 27 were briefed at their bases in Etaples and Montreuil for top cover escort on a bombing mission against London. They rendezvoused over Cap Gris-Nez with Bf 110s of V.*Gruppe* / *(Zerstoerer) Lehrgeschwader* (operational training unit) 1 (V./(Z) LG 1) and ZG 76, together with *Junkers* Ju 88s of KG 77 at around 1000 hours Central European Time (0900 hours BST). *Gefreiter* (Aircraftsman First Class) Hans-Dieter John of 5th *Staffel* /JG 27 followed the Bf 109s of his squadron colleagues across the Channel, climbing towards the cloud cover around 25,000 feet. Below him were the ten Bf 110s of V./(Z) LG 1 and the 13 Bf 110s of ZG 76, together with 15 Ju 88s of KG 77. Effectively, here was a formation of 63 fighters protecting 15 bombers.

With their engine cowlings and rudders painted yellow for easy identification in the confusion of a dogfight, the Bf 109 formation headed towards the English coast. By this stage of the Battle of Britain, the *Luftwaffe's* pilots would have been aware that Fighter Command was back to full strength and probably fully informed by radar plots of the approaching German formation. *Kanalkrankheit,* or "Channel sickness", the all-too-understandable fear of the perilous flight back to base across the unfriendly waters of the Channel, was an ever-present concern and a progressive drain on the morale of all the crews, particularly those in the Bf 109 close escort groups.

A group of Messerschmitt Bf 109s from the 5th Staffel JG 27 are prepared for their next mission in the early part of September 1940. It's unclear whether Gefreiter John's "Black 11" is among these aircraft, but it's possibly one of the machines in the background. (ECC)

After crossing the English coast, the formation was intercepted by Hurricanes of 213 Squadron from Tangmere. Unlike most of his comrades who were soon forced to turn back as their fuel warning lights glowed red, *Gefreiter* John's "Black 11" (*W. Nr.* 3369) was not to return to JG 27's French base. Some reports point to his Bf 109 E-1 being hit by fire from attacking British fighters, either 213 Squadron's Hurricanes or other aircraft from the growing list of RAF squadrons that joined the fight over the Kent and Surrey countryside.

During his interrogation by RAF Intelligence, it was clear that *Gefreiter* John was unaware of being under attack, but something had damaged his radiator and his engine temperature rose sharply. When the engine finally caught fire, he put the aircraft into a steep dive, hoping perhaps to extinguish the flames and make a force-landing. However, the fire continued and he finally had to bale out at 700 feet when it became clear that it was out of control. He landed unhurt, to be interned as a prisoner of war, first in Britain and then later in Canada. He died in May 1941, shortly after his transfer from Britain to Canada.

His aircraft, abandoned and in flames, crashed at 0945 hours in the fields of Mays Farm, Selmeston near Lewes, from where some scraps of wreckage were unearthed by the Wealden Aircraft Archaeological Group in 1976. Some six weeks earlier, this same farm had coincidentally been the site of a crash-landing by another Bf 109, (local casualty No. 2).

10.   Bf 110 C-2 of V./(Z) LG 1 and Hurricane 1 of 249 Squadron crashed on 27th September in Hailsham

As *Gefreiter* John's "Black 11" came to grief at Selmeston, the remainder of the early morning attacking formation had already found it difficult to evade the attentions of the mass of intercepting RAF fighters that had been scrambled by Nos. 10 and 11 Groups. The heavy fighters in the German force were to suffer the most damage, with one of their units virtually decimated well before midday.

Later German accounts of this raid suggest that it was intended as a manoeuvre to draw as many RAF fighters as possible into the air and reduce the fighter strength that could be put up against two other, much larger bombing raids planned for later in the day. This may explain the 4 : 1 ratio of fighters : bombers in the attacking formation. Whatever the aim, the tally of casualties was heavy on both sides by the end of this morning's action. Both Luftwaffe and RAF losses showed that the 27th of September 1940 was as dangerous a day to be in the skies over southern England as any day during the battle, including the 15th of September, Battle of Britain day.

The heavy fighter element of the German formation was made up of two units. Ten Bf 110s of V./(Z) LG 1 were deployed in conjunction with thirteen Bf 110s from II. and III.*Gruppen / ZG* 76. The two units had frequently operated together on bomber escort missions and on this early morning raid they were accompanied by some 40 Bf 109s from I. and II.*Gruppen / JG* 27, giving the formation top cover. The bomber force amounted to 15 *Junkers* Ju 88s from I. *Gruppe /KG* 77, although RAF reports of the raid's strength pointed to a much larger sortie.

For LG 1, the ten aircraft accompanying the bombers represented all the serviceable machines available in the group. On paper, the unit would normally have been able to put 30-40 aircraft in the air but, like many of the heavy fighter units, they had suffered debilitating casualties in the preceding weeks. ZG 76 was also operating all their serviceable aircraft and was down to approximately one third of their theoretical strength.

The twin-engine fighters flew as close escort, some 1,500 ft above the 16,500 ft altitude of the bomber force, while the Bf 109s flew just below the cloud ceiling near 25,000 ft. As the combined formation penetrated towards the Kent/Surrey borders en route to London, the Bf 109 component was harried by RAF fighters and, low on fuel, was soon forced to return to their base in France.

Well aware of the fuel problems of the Bf 109 escorts, Keith Park, AOC of No. 11 Group, directed the attacks against the high cover German fighters soon after crossing the Kent coast, hastening the time when the minds of the Bf 109 pilots became increasingly focussed on their red fuel warning lights. Attacked at this point, the *Jagdwaffe* aircraft were forced to burn fuel at a high rate as they joined combat with the intercepting British fighters and had to return to base all the quicker. This tactic left the bomber and close escort elements of any German attack, usually between 15,000 and 18,000 feet, more vulnerable to both Hurricanes and Spitfires. It was a characteristically intelligent tactic that Keith Park frequently adopted which worked to British advantage.

As a result, when the RAF squadrons finally turned their attention to the bomber force, the two Bf 110 units were the bombers' only fighter cover. Operating in front of the advancing bomber formation, they deployed in their conventional defensive formation circles ("*abwehrkreis*"). Flying in vertically-staggered circles, nose to tail, the heavy fighters acted as a lure to take the attention of the British fighters away from the bombers, at the same time allowing each of the heavy fighters to protect the rear of the aircraft in front.

After twenty minutes over the London area, the 13 aircraft of ZG 76 found their fuel reserves at the limit for safe return to their base at Lisieux, and they broke their circle to dive for the coast. In this type of manoeuvre, the Bf 110 normally had some speed advantage over the Hurricanes that made up the bulk of the defending RAF fighters, and with two exceptions, all 13 aircraft returned to base.

The *Geschwaderadjutant* of II.*Gruppe / ZG* 76, *Oberleutnant* von Eichorn and his *bordfunker, Unteroffizier* Bartmuss, reached the south coast with one engine out of action, only to suffer a cable fire in the fuselage which forced the aircraft down on a comparatively calm sea somewhere off the coast near Hastings. Von Eichorn was badly burned, but after several hours in the water, he was picked up by a British fishing boat which put him ashore at Hastings. *Uffz.* Bartmuss died after he baled out, hitting the water at high speed. Von Eichorn's aircraft had been under attack by two pilots from 249 Squadron, P/O Worrall and Sergeant George Palliser.

A second Bf 110 from III.*Gruppe / ZG* 76 was damaged by the attacks from British fighter and crash-landed at Dieppe. From contemporary accounts and combat reports, the second of these two aircraft had probably been under attack from two other pilots from 249 Squadron, P/O Tom Neil and P/O John Beazley. Both pilots reported attacking and damaging a Bf 110 which was last seen limping out across the Channel after Beazley had broken off wounded by return fire, and Tom Neil had run out of ammunition.

Taken shortly after their move south to North Weald airfield, a group of 249 Squadron pilots pose for the camera with Percy Burton far left. Tom Neil, fifth from the left, is still alive and has appeared regularly on TV programmes covering the Battle of Britain. (AM)

The ten aircraft from LG 1, led by veteran pilot *Hauptmann* Horst Liensberger, the Austrian commander of the group since the middle of April, were not so fortunate. While circling over the Redhill/Horley area, the German fighters came under heavy attack by Hurricanes and Spitfires. With the unusual benefit of height advantage, some of the RAF squadrons dived on the circling German aircraft, attacking head on against the direction of the German defensive circle. Others dived beneath the Bf 110s and climbed to attack their more vulnerable undersurfaces.

Damaged German fighters, unable to maintain their position in the circle, were pounced upon by the gathering RAF fighters. Eventually, all the Bf 110s reached their fuel limits and were obliged to break from the circle in an attempt to reform into groups to make their escape to the coast. By this time however, the bulk of the RAF squadrons scrambled to repel the German force were close in attendance, mainly Hurricanes from both No. 10 and No. 11 Groups. Hurricane units identified in the attacks that followed were 249 Squadron from the sector airfield at North Weald, as well as 1 (RCAF) Squadron and 303 (Polish) Squadron out of Northolt. From the casualty records of the time, it's clear that other Hurricane units also intercepted various elements of the German attacking force. Among these were 17 and 73 Squadrons from Debden, 46 Squadron out of Stapleford Tawney, 213 Squadron from Exeter, together with 253 and 501 Squadrons from Kenley. Spitfire units involved included 72 and 92 Squadrons out of Biggin Hill, and 602 Squadron from Westhampnett.

The beginning of the Blitz : 7th - 30th September

Contemporary records show a trail of seven Bf 110s from LG 1 that crashed through the Surrey and Sussex countryside. Oxted, Gatwick, Chelwood Gate, Heathfield, Horam and finally Hailsham, all witnessed aircraft from the group falling victim mostly to the guns of the various Hurricanes, although one was brought down by AA fire.

Hauptmann Liensberger managed to escape as far south as Hailsham, before finally meeting his destiny in the form of a 249 Squadron Hurricane. He and his *bordfunker, Unteroffizier*

Albert Koepge, had been hotly pursued all the way from the Redhill/Gatwick area by a 21-year old South African pilot, Flying Officer Percival Ross-Frame Burton.

Gruppenkommandeur Horst Liensberger with the unit's battered Mercedes staff car in Brussels in happier times. (CGC)

After Liensberger dived out of the defensive circle over the Redhill area, both the German aircraft and his pursuer were soon flying at tree-top height, jinking to avoid hills and other obstacles, following the contours of the land as the German veteran tried to prevent F/O Burton getting a clear shot. Witnesses who saw the chase ducked as the planes lifted up to avoid trees and buildings, branches swaying furiously in the wash of their propellers, and spent cartridges cases pinging off road surfaces.

Finally, just north of Hailsham, Burton's guns fell silent, apparently out of ammunition. After passing St. Mary's Church tower in the centre of the town, with the Hurricane slightly above and behind the Bf 110, locals saw the British aircraft bank and dive in what appeared to be another attacking pass. Suddenly, both machines lurched upwards, with the starboard wingtip of the Hurricane and the complete tail assembly of the Bf 110 spiralling to earth.

The collision has been explained by a variety of theories but, like many such occurrences in the heat of action, the real cause may never be clear. Burton's colleagues from 249 Squadron maintain that, mortally wounded and out of ammunition, his determination to stop the German aircraft from making its escape caused him to use his own aircraft's wing to force the Bf 110 into the ground. Flying at a height probably of less than 100 feet and at 250 mph, this would have certainly been suicidally brave.

Sergeant George Palliser, one of Burton's nearby squadron colleagues, heard Burton announce over the radio that he had been mortally wounded and, since he didn't expect to be able to make it back to base, he was determined to stop the German aircraft escaping. Some reports from the local people who discovered Burton's body after the crash suggested that he had numerous bullet wounds, but there was no post mortem to confirm this.

An alternative theory is that Liensberger, with his relentless pursuer still behind, realised Burton was out of ammunition. Since he was then less than five miles from the coast, he may have decided to try to lose Burton's Hurricane, at least temporarily, by suddenly pulling up and simultaneously reducing speed. He may have also hoped that the British aircraft would overshoot and present itself as a target for his own powerful, forward-firing armament.

It was well known among German airmen that both the Spitfire and the Hurricane were armed with eight Browning .303 inch machine guns, but they only carried 15 seconds of ammunition. Most British fighter pilots during the Battle of Britain soon ran out of ammunition as enthusiasm in the heat of the action frequently made it difficult to limit bursts of fire to just one or two seconds duration. It was a very accurate aerial gunner that consistently managed such a skill.

The Bf 110 on the other hand had a battery of four 7.9 mm machine guns firing forward, each with 1,000 rounds of ammunition, giving them almost 60 seconds of continuous firing. This was in addition to the aircraft's two forward firing 20 mm cannons that could either be fired independently, or at the same time as the machine guns. The cannons had almost 18 seconds of firing duration with magazines holding 180 rounds for each gun. The aircraft's *bordfunker* also operated another machine gun facing towards the rear with a number of replacement magazines.

However much Percy Burton may have conserved his ammunition, the disparity between the ammunition capacity of the British and German fighters would have worked against him during the frantic pursuit from Redhill to Hailsham. Doubtless, whatever the state of his wounds, Burton would have been preferred to have been able to fire a further two second burst of 320 rounds, rather than ramming the German aircraft.

The bulk of the mangled wreckage of Horst Liensberger's Messerschmitt Bf 110 came to rest in Simmon's Field south of Hailsham. (MP)

Some members of Liensberger's unit heard a brief radio message from their *Gruppenkommandeur,* reporting that he had lost power in both engines and needed to make a force-landing. The radio transmission was cut off suddenly, arguably as the two aircraft collided, perhaps as he used the last of his airspeed to gain height to look for a suitable site to land his aircraft.

Whatever the reason, the two aircraft struck with fatal results for all three airmen. With no tail assembly, Liensberger's machine tumbled forward and ploughed into what was then known as Simmon's Field, between Mill Road and Station Road in Hailsham, with one of the torn-off engines finishing up in a field behind Hamlin's Mill. The severed tail assembly, complete with four victory roundels recording the pilot's tally of kills, lay in Simmon's Field with the top of the starboard fin showing the damage caused by the Hurricane's impact.

Hauptmann Liensberger, still strapped into his seat, was thrown clear of the wreckage in the aircraft's final agonised manoeuvres, with some eyewitness suggesting that his parachute had partly deployed. The position of the body of Albert Koepge is unclear, with logic and some observers saying he was also thrown clear. Other eyewitnesses suggested his body was trapped in the wreckage of the rear cockpit. Eyewitnesses who arrived on the scene soon after the crash remarked on the lack of apparent injuries to the pilot, but a much later post-mortem showed he had broken a thigh bone and had some injuries to his jaw. Their bodies were buried in Hailsham cemetery on the 2nd of October, together with several of their comrades from other LG 1 aircraft that fell nearby in Sussex. They were later exhumed for re-burial, Liensberger in his hometown of Innsbruck, Austria, and Koepge in the German War Graves Commission cemetery in Cannock Chase, Staffordshire.

Some distance from the main wreckage of Horst Liensberger's aircraft lies the severed tail assembly, showing clear signs of the damage caused by the collision with Percy Burton's Hurricane. (MP)

Percy Burton never regained sufficient control of his Hurricane (V6683). With its engine at full throttle, it slammed into a large oak tree in the fields south of New Barn Farm, throwing the pilot clear as the machine broke up and caught fire, scattering a stream of burning high octane fuel over the surrounding fields. A small plaque still marks the site of the aircraft's crash, and was the location for the local RAF Association to hold an annual remembrance ceremony until a few years ago.

The pilot's body, parachute partially deployed, was found in a nearby ditch by David Cottington, a local farm worker, and moved along with those of the German airmen to the local mortuary. On the 30th of September, Percy Burton's body was transferred by train from Hailsham to Chichester for burial at Tangmere, where his is one of many graves marked by a simple headstone in this quiet country churchyard, many miles from his native South Africa. He was not to receive the Victoria Cross that many felt he deserved for his actions on the 27th of September 1940, but he did receive a posthumous mention in despatches some 18 months later, the official attitude being that there were no service witnesses to what actually happened.

In the cemetery behind Tangmere Church lies the simple grave marker for South African Percy Burton, regarded by many of his squadron colleagues as deserving the VC rather than the simple "mention in despatches" that he was posthumously awarded later in the war.

It still surprises me that during the whole of the Battle of Britain, only one RAF fighter pilot was to receive the VC, this being one of F/O Burton's 249 Squadron colleagues, Flight Lieutenant James Nicholson, for heroism in action over Southampton on the 16th of August 1940. The fact that this pilot was also from 249 Squadron was thought by some to be another factor preventing F/O Burton being awarded the VC.

When part of the land near where the crashes occurred was being developed for housing in 1980, Hailsham Council, supported by local aircraft historian Andy Saunders, decided that it would be appropriate to name one of the paths on the housing estate after the South African pilot. Few perhaps have the slightest idea today why part of the estate bears the name "Burton Walk" in his memory. Fewer still would find it easy today to understand either the brave rage, or the emergency manoeuvre that caused Percy Burton to ram the German machine and stop it escaping back across the Channel.

By the end of the morning, only three of the ten Bf 110s from LG 1 flying on this sortie managed to return to base at Ligescourt in France, the others having been shot down or crash-landed in southern England. With only two crews remaining from their strength at the start of the French campaign in May 1940, the unit was effectively withdrawn from operations over England and reformed as one of the *Luftwaffe's* first night fighter units, I./*Nachtjagdgeschwader* (NJG) 3, flying Bf 110s equipped as night fighters in defence of Germany.

An intriguing side note to the events over southern England during the early part of the 27th of September relates to the intended purpose claimed for the German attack. This early sortie was arguably aimed at weakening the ability of RAF Fighter Command to counter two later, larger German attacks which were planned around midday and during the afternoon.

Analysing the casualty records for the morning raid and even taking account of the virtual decimation of V./(Z)LG 1, the *Luftwaffe* lost eight Bf 110s (one from ZG 76), one Bf 109 and four *Junkers* Ju 88 medium bombers, with 19 dead and 12 airmen taken prisoners of war. Only six Hurricanes and four Spitfires were destroyed with nine pilots killed in action, but this also left a further 14 Hurricanes and five Spitfires with various levels of damage and three pilots wounded. While 17 pilots among the British aircraft casualties came out of the action unhurt, a total of 29

British fighter aircraft were removed from the game as far as the later German raids were concerned. Some of the damaged aircraft may have been repaired in time to fly again that day and, by the end of September, aircraft deliveries from the factories and repair units were at a high level. However, it's likely that the German raids later in the day probably did not suffer as much as they might have done without the raid in the morning.

Percy Burton (right) with Irish colleague, Jimmy Meaker, who was also killed later the same day, baling out of his Hurricane over Dallington and striking his aircraft's tail. (AM)

Despite the exaggerated claims made by both sides at the time, subsequent evaluation of actual losses shows that, after the disastrous casualties suffered by the *Luftwaffe* on the 15th of September, the 27th of September was the day when both British and German losses neared the peak suffered in the middle of the month. From the end of September, the heavy

Luftwaffe losses during daylight missions over England effectively forced a further tactical switch away from daylight bombing to night bombing. From the beginning of October, most *Luftwaffe* bombing operations during the day were restricted to Bf 109 and Bf 110 fighter-bombers.

11.   Bf 109 E-1 of JG 54 crash-landed on 30th September at Rockhouse Bank near Norman's Bay

September came to an end with the weather on a fair note, accompanied by some cloud and light winds. The 30th of September was the last day that the *Luftwaffe* was to mount daylight bombing raids on southern Britain on the sort of scale that had become commonplace since the second week of August. From the beginning of October, the German bomber fleets that were suffering so badly in daylight attacks left most of their sorties against Britain till after dark. At least during the night, they were less at risk from fighter attack, the main threat being from anti-aircraft fire, spectacular, though notoriously ineffective as a general rule.

The end of the month saw the *Luftwaffe* suffering the greatest number of single engine fighter losses on any one day during the Battle of Britain. No less than 28 Bf 109s were brought down, the equivalent strength of two full *Staffeln*. Three of these came to land around the Eastbourne area and another two were shot down in the sea off Beachy Head and Newhaven. The bulk of the losses however were simply listed as "missing", in most cases a euphemism for aircraft that disappeared over the Channel, struggling back alone to France low on fuel or with battle damage.

The morning saw a classic wartime cock-up, which underlined the careful balance that the escort fighters were forced to maintain between their need to conserve fuel and the bombers' need for protection. Various *Jagdwaffe* groups were detailed to escort *Junkers* Ju 88 bombers from II.*Gruppe*/ KG 30 sent on a mission against London. The bombers were to find their target using the radio direction system code-named *Knickebein*, which projected one radio beam for the bombers to follow on a course for their target, with a second beam sent from a different transmitter, bisecting the first beam over the target location. Somehow, the lead bomber missed the second beam and flew some distance beyond London, which was obscured by cloud. They didn't turn for home until the fighter escort was painfully low on fuel.

The fighters, mindful of Goering's dissatisfaction with the effectiveness of their defence of the bombers to date, had been unwilling to break away since the bombers were under constant attack from groups of British fighters. To make matters worse, the German bomber commander chose to follow a homeward route via the Isle of Wight instead of Dover, leaving the fighters with a long sea crossing to make landfall in France.

According to Ulrich Steinhilper, one of the escorting pilots from JG 52, after the bombers were finally safe from British fighter attack, the escorts flew at sea level in a desperate attempt to conserve enough fuel to get back to home base. As a result of the bomber commander's blunder, as many as 19 German fighter pilots were listed as missing that day, with a high probability that most had been forced to ditch in the Channel out of fuel. The commander of the bomber group was later court-martialled.

Shortly after 1300 hours, a major raid developed with one group of 18 German fighters crossing the coast at Lympne, operating on an offensive sweep (*freie Jagd*). These were followed by some 100 other aircraft, mostly Bf 109s and Bf 110s, escorting *Junkers* Ju 88 and *Dornier* Do 17 bombers. Other fighters were later sent to patrol off the Dover coast to act as escorts for the returning bombers. Most of the bombers were turned back 20 miles from central London, but a handful of Ju 88s, accompanied by some Bf 109s, managed to reach the capital.

Aircraft from JG 54, operating from Guines, were among the Bf 109s in this raid. This was a recently-formed unit, amalgamating parts of other disbanded squadrons. One of these was the 7th *Staffel* / JG 54, which had previously operated as the 3rd *Staffel* / JG 21. Their aircraft carried a unit emblem depicting a winged clog on either side of the engine cowling, in recognition of time previously spent based in Holland.

Unteroffizier Fritz Marcks was part of the 7th *Staffel*, flying a Bf 109 E-1, "White 4" (*W. Nr.* 6050). Along with his squadron colleagues, he took off from his base in northern France soon after midday. Approaching London at about 19,000 feet, the raid was intercepted by groups of British fighters. With liquid-cooled engines like all the front line fighters operating over southern England at the time, his Bf 109 E-1 depended on the radiator system operating efficiently to maintain power. Reflecting the fortunes of many other German fighter pilots, Marcks was unfortunate enough to be hit in the all-important coolant system of his DB 601 engine, and the engine temperature rapidly rose to 120 degrees C. It soon caught fire, by which time he had lost a lot of height and was flying too low to bale out, so a crash-landing was the only solution. On landing at Rock House Banks, near Norman's Bay outside Pevensey, he lost no time in getting out of the aircraft for fear of fire and explosion, and was soon taken prisoner of war.

From the unit records, this aircraft had been attacked by a Spitfire over Dover, and was classed as a write-off after the landing, but it hasn't been possible to identify which RAF pilot was involved in the attack that led to this casualty.

In his interrogation by RAF Intelligence, Marcks revealed he had been a civilian pilot on the German Air Force reserve list before the war and had been called up on war's outbreak. Underlining the shortage of pilots that were needed to maintain the required escort numbers for the *Luftwaffe* daylight bombing missions over England, he had been flying sorties practically every day for the previous two weeks. He had benefited from few rest days and had been given no leave since sometime the previous June.

12.   Bf 109 E-4 of JG 53 crash-landed on 30th September at Langney

Less than ten minutes after Fritz Marcks emerged from his machine near Norman's Bay, the flat land to the east of Eastbourne saw another Bf 109 ploughing a furrow across rough pastureland at Langney. Shortly after 1400 hours, *Feldwebel* Walter Scholz was forced to land his *Messerschmitt* Bf 109 E-4, "Yellow 13" (*W. Nr.* 1325). He'd run out of fuel on a bomber escort mission as part of the 3rd *Staffel* / JG 53, and the newspapers of the time of course made great play on the "unlucky number 13" theme.

When I first read about this particular casualty of the battle, the fact that the aircraft had run out of fuel made me jump to what seemed a logical conclusion. Scholz, like many Bf 109 pilots escorting bombers on London missions, had probably become involved in dog-fighting with British fighters somewhere over Kent or Surrey and had used more fuel than would allow him safe passage back to France. However, the actual circumstances are slightly more bizarre.

By this stage of the war, with London the main target for daylight German bomber sorties, Bf 109s that stayed with their bombers over London faced serious problems with fuel, putting to one side the more potent dangers of waiting Hurricanes and Spitfires.

The German single engine fighter had normally used approximately one-third of its fuel by the time it crossed the British coast inbound, assuming it had not wasted fuel over Calais waiting to rendezvous with the bombers, not an uncommon experience. This meant that over the docks and the east end of London, these fighters had no more than 10-15 minutes of fuel duration before they would be forced to turn for home and safely regain their bases in northern France. Any combat with throttles pushed to their limits would either reduce the time they could stay with the bombers, or risk the outcome that affected many Bf 109 aircraft, a crash-landing out of fuel either in Britain or, with luck, on the beaches of northern France. The other alternative, ditching in the Channel, was more difficult to contemplate, but it had already clearly become the fate of several unfortunate Bf 109 pilots on the 30th of September, a constant nagging fear that continually affected *Jagdwaffe* morale.

Involved in the same raid as the Bf 109 that had previously force-landed near Norman's Bay some ten minutes earlier, *Feldwebel* Scholz and his 3rd *Staffel* colleagues had left their base at Etaples in France to form part of the bomber close escort group. During his interrogation, Scholz claimed to have rendezvoused with the bombers between 18,000 and 19,000 feet over the Channel, not far from the English coast, but he soon found his fuel tank was almost empty. Since other aircraft from the same escort group don't seem to have had the same problem, it's clear there was something unusual about Scholz' situation.

Under guard in the marshy fields of Langney, "Yellow 13", Feldwebel Scholz' Messerschmitt Bf 109 E-4 from the 3rd Staffel JG 53, waits for RAF Intelligence personnel to investigate the wreck. (TRB)

It's difficult to imagine that his fuel tank had not been filled to the same capacity as all of his comrades, so it's probable there was another reason behind the force-landing that became his only practical choice. He was marginally too low to attempt a gliding return across the Channel, something that was more feasible from a height of around 21,500 feet, another drawback of the high wing loading of Willy Messerschmitt's Bf 109 design. For aircraft like "Yellow 13", operating in the close escort group around the bombers at 18,000 to 19,000 feet, this option was impractical.

There must have been another explanation why Scholz' aircraft ran out of fuel. His statement reflects that he had come directly from his base to the rendezvous point with the bomber formation, so he should have had sufficient fuel under normal circumstances at least to reach London and return safely to France. The truth may lie in the findings of the RAF crash report, which identified various bullet strikes in both the engine compartment and the cooling system of the aircraft.

Scholz was adamant that he had not been in combat prior to exhausting his fuel, but it's not impossible that he may have been the unknowing target of some stray burst of fire perhaps from a British fighter he didn't see or hear. If he had been the target of an unknown attacker chancing a long range burst of fire from below, damage to his fuel tank and the resulting fuel loss would have been entirely possible. At the height he was flying, ground fire from small arms would not have been a factor, but it was not unknown for an unseen adversary to unleash a long range burst of fire from a distance and make some lucky strikes.

Shortly before Scholz' aircraft came down at Langney, one of his comrades from the 4th *Staffel* /JG 53 was also shot down, crashing "White 3" (*W. Nr.* 6384) into the sea off Beachy Head. *Unteroffizier* Karl Michael Vogel had been escorting the bombers en route to London when his formation was intercepted over the Tunbridge Wells area. He claimed during his interrogation by RAF Intelligence that he had not been hit by enemy fire, although his engine had seized. While he was hopefully heading for home in his Bf 109 E-1 with a dead engine, he was shot down at 1350 hours by a lone Spitfire. The German pilot was fortunate to have been rescued after spending some two hours in the water. He was picked up by a British destroyer and taken to Portsmouth where he became a prisoner of war.

13.   Bf 109 E-4 of JG 26 crash-landed on 30th September at East Dean

This particular aircraft is now on display in the Battle of Britain hangar at the Imperial War Museum in Duxford, partly renovated in a diorama depicting the plane after it crash-landed on the 30th of September 1940. The crash site lies less than 1,000 metres east of where I live today, on the southeast limits of the village of East Dean, some 4 miles west of Eastbourne and just over a mile from the Channel coast.

A recent view of a more populated East Dean taken from the approximate spot where the Duxford Messerschmitt Bf 109 finished up after its crash-landing at the end of September 1940.

Like a number of Bf 109s that survived their landings virtually intact, this Bf 109 was sent on a public tour overseas to generate financial and political support for the war effort. In doing so, it became one of the most widely-travelled Bf 109s in existence, having finished its tour in 1941 by crossing the Atlantic, where it was put on display in several American and Canadian cities as part of the "Bundles for Britain" campaign.

Various other German casualties of the summer 1940 conflict were displayed during the war as far afield as South Africa, Australia and New Zealand. The aim of this was to encourage Commonwealth and other countries in their support of Britain during those lonely early years of the war before the official entry of the United States as an active participant after Pearl Harbour. None of these other examples appear to have survived as long as the aircraft on display at Duxford.

After the war, the East Dean Bf 109 finished up with the Canadian Amprior Research Establishment in Ontario, by which time souvenir hunters had rendered the remains apparently beyond repair. Nevertheless, the remnants were eventually purchased by a group of British enthusiasts in 1961 and brought back to Britain for renovation in November 1966. In all probability, it was this development that produced the "Flying Review" article that I recall from my youth, the timing being about right. Peter Foote was involved in the aircraft's first restoration programme at Hurn Airport near Bournemouth, but for many reasons, most probably financial, the private sector renovation was never completed. In March 1988, the aircraft was obtained by the Imperial War Museum, which used National Heritage Memorial Funds to restore the machine to its current condition.

During the closing stages of the Battle of Britain in September and October 1940, the aircraft had been assigned to II.*Gruppe*/ JG 26 (*Schlageter*), based at Marquise-Est, inland from Cap Gris-Nez in northern France.

Adolf Galland, arguably one of the most well-known figures from the history of German fighter pilots during World War Two, was posted to JG 26 in early June 1940 and led III.*Gruppe*/ JG 26 as *Major* (Squadron Leader), until being given command of the whole *Geschwader* on the 22nd of August 1940. Anxious to maintain his position among the leading aces of the time, he succeeded in annoying Goering by trying to refuse this promotion since he feared more ground duties would cut into his flying hours. Galland appears to have had almost as much talent for annoying the *Reichsmarschall* as he obviously had for shooting down Allied aircraft.

Famously, Goering later berated Galland, Werner Moelders (the commander of JG 51) and other unit commanders for the losses his bomber groups were suffering and asked them what they needed to protect the bombers more effectively. Moelders is said to have opted for all of his Bf 109s to be equipped with the more powerful Daimler Benz DB 601N engine. Already antagonised by Goering's criticisms of his fighter pilots' aggressiveness, Galland controversially asked for his unit to be equipped with Spitfires. His logic was that the Spitfire's unique elliptical wing made them better able to manoeuvre at low speed because of their lower wing loading compared to the Bf 109, making them more suited to the close escort role that Goering was demanding.

However such outspoken comments may have infuriated the pompous *Reichsmarschall*, he would have found it difficult to deal too harshly with Galland who, with Werner Moelders and Helmut Wick of JG 2, was fast assuming celebrity status within both the *Luftwaffe* and in the eyes of the German public. German fighter tactics generally favoured the leader of each formation, whether as small as a "*rotte*" (pair), or as large as a whole "*Geschwader*" (Group). In this way, the leaders were the pilots who built up the higher victory tallies and therefore progressively became the target of the German publicity machine and public admiration. Galland became particularly notorious for his aggressive efforts to stay at the top of the aces' scoreboard, at the same time demanding the recognition that went with this.

Having survived the war to die as recently as 1996, Adolf Galland may be the more easily recognised of these three German aces today. At the time, all three were suffering from what loosely translates as "throat ache", eagerly searching out victims in the air in a race to be awarded ever-more prestigious laurels to their Iron Cross status. Neither Wick nor Moelders survived the war. Wick was shot down and posted missing off the Isle of Wight some two months later. Withdrawn from front line operations and promoted to the *Luftwaffe's* Inspector of Fighters, Moelders became the victim of engine failure during deteriorating weather in a He 111 bomber on a domestic flight near Breslau in Germany in November 1941. He had been flying from the Russian Front in order to attend the funeral of Ernst Udet who had committed suicide.

Smoking his signature cigar, Adolf Galland with some JG 26 colleagues in front of one of his personal aircraft showing its distinctive "Mickey Mouse" emblem beneath the cockpit.

Both within the *Jagdwaffe* and through the German propaganda machine, the *Luftwaffe* had perpetuated the role of the fighter aces (*experten*) in the image of the "Knights of the Air" from World War One, reflecting the reputations of the aces from that earlier period. Two decades earlier, pilots such as Manfred von Richthofen, Oswald Boelcke, Ernst Udet and even Hermann Goering himself had achieved celebrity status through their prowess over the Western Front. With both Goering and Udet pivotally involved in the creation of the *Luftwaffe* during the 1930s, it was no surprise that the new aces found themselves groomed for stardom as the ultimate hunter/killers of the new era. Galland and Moelders, jokingly compared themselves to their heroes from World War One. Moelders was happy to see himself as Boelcke, viewed as the great tactician of earlier aerial fighting, while Galland was pleased to take on the mantle of Richthofen, the greatest ace.

By contrast, in the early stages of the war, British Fighter Command was at pains to take almost the opposite approach. In order to foster the concept of unit identity, the stress was on group rather than individual achievements. While individual victory claims were assessed, the emphasis was more on confirming the result of damage to enemy forces, rather than boosting individual scores.

RAF fighting tactics took the form of formation attacks against bomber formations, with each pilot making successive passes at the target. With only eight rifle calibre machine guns per aircraft, destruction of well-armoured bombers by a single attacker was possible, but probably the exception. More frequently, a German bomber casualty would generally be attacked by a number of British fighters, each claiming a portion of the kill. In this way, even the well-known personalities among the Battle of Britain fighter pilots amassed comparatively modest numbers of kills when compared with the stars of the *Jagdwaffe*. It was not until the end of the Battle of Britain that the RAF started to react to the demands of a thirsty newspaper industry by giving them access to the pilots that had achieved ace status in defending Britain.

On the 30th of September 1940, there were four main German raids aimed at London spread throughout the day, with two further attacks directed at targets in the south western sector. The largest of these raids crossed the Kent coast around 1600 hours heading towards London and its suburbs.

Junkers Ju 88s and *Heinkel* He 111s from KG 77 were sent to bomb the London area with a heavy fighter escort which included Adolf Galland's JG 26. It was a mission that would leave JG 26 with comparatively heavy casualties. The *Stab* (Headquarters) flight lost *Hauptmann* Walter Kienzle, Galland's wingman, in a dogfight with Hurricanes of No. 303 (Polish) Squadron south of London, as they fought to keep the attacking RAF fighters away from the bombers. The 7th and 9th *Staffeln* lost a total of three aircraft, with two pilots killed and one wounded. The Bf 109 that came down at East Dean was the fifth casualty of this evening mission.

In the cockpit of "White 4" (*W. Nr.* 1190) was 22-year old *Unteroffizier* Horst Perez, only recently attached to the 4th *Staffel*. Despite his recent arrival, he was fortunate enough to have been assigned one of the upgraded Bf 109s with the more powerful DB 601N engine, capable of 1,200 hp for take-off at 2,600 rpm compared with the rating for the standard DB 601 engine of 1,175 hp at 2,480 rpm.

When he made the crash-landing on the fields above East Dean, "White 4" carried five victory bars (*Abschussbalken*) on the aircraft's fin, theoretically denoting the pilot's record of kills. In fact, the victories these recorded were actually achieved by II.*Gruppe's* former *Gruppenkommandeur*, Karl Ebbighausen, who had been posted missing on the 16th of August while flying in a different Bf 109 E-4. As *Gruppenkommandeur*, Ebbighausen probably had the use of more than one aircraft, depending on which was serviceable for operations. When he crashed in the sea some six miles off Dover, it's likely that *W. Nr.* 1190 was being given a field upgrade by changing the engine for the more powerful DB 601N unit, as well as various other technical improvements.

With an actual tally of seven victories by the time he was posted as missing, Ebbighausen had then been leading the *Stab* (Headquarters) Flight of II.*Gruppe*/ JG 26 on an offensive sweep (*freie Jagd*) with four other pilots, including Eckhardt Roch, Waldi Maerz and Karl Borris. Soon after midday, they were attacked from above by seven Spitfires of 266 Squadron from Hornchurch. This squadron had been transferred into No. 11 Group only a week earlier, during which time they had already lost three pilots.

It appears that they were yet another well-trained squadron that lacked the battle awareness required to survive in the hectic southeast that summer. As they dived on Ebbighausen's formation, they failed to check above and behind and were bounced in turn by more Bf 109s from above. Joined by this second group of Bf 109s, the German pilots succeeded in dominating the engagement, and 266 Squadron finished up with five aircraft lost, one damaged, three pilots killed and two wounded. Ebbighausen became the only recorded German casualty of this action, his aircraft crashing into the sea, curiously unseen by his colleagues.

266 Squadron was soon moved from Hornchurch back to Wittering in Leicestershire in No. 12 Group to recuperate from its losses. It's a curious coincidence that 266 Squadron was at the time the squadron of Sergeant Donald Ernest Kingaby, the pilot credited with bringing "White 4" down at East Dean on the 30th of September, although there is no record of his being involved in this earlier action off Dover.

After Ebbighausen was posted missing in mid August, *W. Nr.* 1190 was given a new aircraft identification number, "White 4", and was made available to other pilots of the 4th *Staffel*. The

"Tiger's Head" emblem, carried on the port fuselage side under the rear edge of the cockpit, had been designed earlier by Ebbighausen and the 4th *Staffel* used it as a mark of respect for him. It's ironic that our local pub in East Dean, near where the aircraft force-landed, is actually called "The Tiger", as it had for centuries before World War Two.

The "Tiger's Head" unit emblem of the 4th Staffel JG 26 renovated on the Duxford Messerschmitt using the faded original evident when the Imperial War Museum took over the project. It's unclear whether the bullet holes under the cockpit rim were the result of aerial combat or, more likely, ground fire after the crash-landing.

Perez had left Marquise, crossing the English coast near Eastbourne at a height of between 16,000 and 18,000 feet, where he and his comrades turned northwards to rendezvous with the assigned bomber formation returning from London. The unit failed to contact the bombers, and circled north of Eastbourne in the hope of meeting up with them before their fuel reserves became too low. Here, they were intercepted by Spitfires from 92 Squadron and, during the dogfight that followed, Perez broke off and headed for the coast and home. However, he was attacked by one of the Spitfires, possibly flown by Sergeant Kingaby.

While he was comparatively new to 92 Squadron, having joined the unit only at the beginning of September, Sergeant Kingaby's time with 266 Squadron would have given him a level of combat maturity that probably afforded him some advantage over the apparently inexperienced Perez. Kingaby was a vicar's son, who had been educated at King's, Ely, before joining up. He went on to finish the war with a tally of kills including 22 and a half confirmed, eight probably destroyed and 16 damaged, making him No. 22 in the post war list of the RAF's top fighter aces.

Contrast this with the 107 kills attributed to Adolf Galland, or the 275 kills of Gunther Rall, Germany's third highest scoring fighter pilot. The top scoring German fighter pilot of the war, Erich "Bubi" Hartmann, who became operational in 1942 on the eastern front, ended the war with 352 kills, all in the eastern theatre. He remains the top scoring fighter pilot of all time. Having survived the war, he served 10 years hard labour in Russia and died at the age of 72 in Germany.

Sergeant Kingaby's brief combat report as Green 2 at 1700 hours on the 30th of September is short and to the point, describing an attack on what could possibly have been Perez' Bf 109.

I encountered 2 109s at 8,000 ft north of Lewes and carried out a quarter attack on the leader. I gave him a four second burst and heavy black smoke came from his engine. The other 109 attacked me and I broke off the contact. No damage to my aircraft.

In looking through the 92 Squadron combat reports that have survived at the Public Records Office at Kew, it's possible that another pilot from this unit may have been the cause of Perez' forced landing at East Dean. As has already been clear from many of the combat descriptions that have formed the background to this book, pilot recollections of frequently frantic action rarely gave a very clear picture. The combat report of P/O J.F. Drummond showed some interesting similarities to the circumstances that probably led to "White 4" landing not far from Beachy Head. Flying in 92 Squadron's "A" flight on the evening of the 30th of September, P/O Drummond described an encounter with some 50 Bf 109s over Brighton.

As Yellow 1, I was on patrol with the squadron at 27,000 feet NW of Brighton. We sighted about 50 me 109s above us.
We went into line astern and sighted 15 bombers about 10,000 feet below. We dived down to attack.
On the way down, I encountered 10 109s. I fired a burst at the leader and broke away. I saw 2 Me 109s at 20,000 feet and attacked from the quarter and below, firing a four second burst from 350 yards.
White smoke came from the exhaust of the 109 and he began to lose height. I was attacked by 2 more 109s, fired one burst and then broke away.
I last saw the damaged 109 losing height in the direction of Beachy Head.

The passing of nearly seven decades makes it impossible to identify whether Kingaby or Drummond was the real cause of the aircraft coming down.

After taking hits in the fuselage around the cockpit area and the port wing, Perez suffered engine failure, a normal sign of battle damage to the coolant or oil system for this type of fighter. "White smoke" from the exhaust manifolds or radiator was a telltale signature of damage to the coolant system. "Black smoke" was often caused by a Messerschmitt pilot ramming open the throttle to get maximum performance from the fuel-injected Daimler Benz engine. It could also signify damage to the engine's oil system.

In his short combat report, Don Kingaby described attacking the lead aircraft of a *rotte*, but bearing in mind Horst Perez had only recently arrived in JG 26, it's difficult to believe he had already become a *rottenfuehrer*, rather than a wingman, protecting his leader from behind. P/O Drummond also recalled his last sighting of the aircraft he had damaged losing height on a track from somewhere north of Brighton towards Beachy Head, so it's not impossible this was actually Perez' "White 4". Drummond was sadly killed when he baled out too low after a collision with another Spitfire over Tangmere on the 10th of October 1940 while both aircraft were attacking a *Dornier* Do 17. Don Kingaby survived the war, but he is also no longer with us.

Ground crew from 92 Squadron work on one of the unit's Spitfires, topping up the aircraft's header fuel tank and adjusting the pilot's parachute harness in preparation for the next sortie.

At the end of September 1940, the fields on the South Downs had long been harvested and, as a defence against glider landings by German troops, wire barriers were strung on poles across these open areas, making any landing a hazardous undertaking. In the event, after flying over East Dean, Perez managed to land "White 4" in a stubble field on Crapham Down, luckily finding a safe route between the rows of poles in a wheels-up landing that caused relatively minor damage to the aircraft. On landing however, Perez was shot in the hand and jaw by British troops from a nearby anti-aircraft battery, before being arrested by local police.

Jesse Taylor, who has lived his whole life in the village of East Dean, apart from during his national service in the 1950s, recalled the day the German aircraft came down in a letter sent to the Imperial War Museum. He's now in his late 70s and a village council member who is happy to talk of his life in the village and the adventures he and his friends had during the war years.

I was ten years old at the time and war through the eyes of a young boy was quite exciting. On spotting the aircraft, life became more exciting as it was an Me 109. It flew right over the village quite low and kept circling for about thirty minutes, when suddenly it came over very low and belly flopped in a field half a mile away. All the open areas had pylons erected with cables running between them. This was to stop the landing of aircraft of any kind, so it was a masterpiece of navigation for this pilot to get under the cables and not collide with the pylons.

The pilot climbed out of his aircraft only to be confronted by a British Policeman and men from the Homeguard and a group of young boys. I remember vividly the maroon and white spotted scarf he was wearing. There was also blood coming from one of his hands.

Jesse had earlier been on the village green with his friend Tony Cheale, coincidentally a step-brother of one of my own school friends during my youth in the village. They had seen the German fighter circling nearby and as it came lower over the downs to the east, they rushed excitedly up the Eastbourne Road to see what had happened. In doing so, they beat the local policeman, Constable Harry Hyde, up to the site where Horst Perez was captured. Jesse recalls the pilot as a tall, dark-haired man, possibly wearing some sort of decoration around his neck. He also sadly recalled that someone at the crash site stole the pilot's watch, a gift from his mother, something that was not an unusual occurrence when German pilots were captured.

John Surtees, a well-known local historian, recounts the call to "String 'im up" coming from Mrs. Dooley, a local widow who had lost her husband during the 1914-1918 war. Fortunately for Horst Perez, she was in the minority and within a short space of time, he was enjoying a cup of tea, courtesy of the constable Harry Hyde's wife in the police house, in those days a few doors away from the local church.

Other recollections of the afternoon of the 30th of September reveal a similar picture.

The aircraft came down in a nearby field adjacent to the Eastbourne Road. The pilot made a perfect wheels-up landing. He tried to make a run for it and was shot at by gunners from a nearby Ack-Ack Battery.

Hands in the air, even to me he looked quite young. I wondered what he made of the oddly assorted column behind him. First there was PC Hyde with a revolver held in the pilot's back, he was followed by a few members of the Local Defence Volunteers, they in turn were followed by men from the Auxiliary Fire Service. A lady in front of me could speak German and she spoke to the pilot. She asked him what he thought about being a prisoner of war and the war being over for him. He replied that he was not too concerned as the war would be over soon and he would be released – something that was taken to imply that he expected the invasion to take place shortly and that he would be on the winning side.

These comments suggest Perez was much more confident than he had reason to be, given the circumstances of his capture. However, the Air Intelligence report on his interrogation pointed to an understandable sense of uncertainty, which belied the confidence suggested by comments made above. He expressed concern over the fate of colleagues from his own 4th *Staffel* / JG 26, as well as I.*Gruppe*/ LG 1, which also flew Bf 109s from a base in the Calais area. After a period of internment in Britain, he joined many of his *Luftwaffe* colleagues in POW camps in Canada, where he remained for the duration of the war.

Jabos by day, bombers at night:
1st - 31st October

The closing days of September witnessed the last major daylight raids on Britain. The resilience of RAF Fighter Command and its ability to respond with growing intensity to daylight *Luftwaffe* bombing sorties finally persuaded German *OKL* that a further change of direction in its campaign against Britain was required.

With the British government clearly now determined to fight rather than sue for a peaceful settlement, and with any invasion of Britain during 1940 now impractical as autumn began, Hitler was content to give Goering's *Luftwaffe* free rein in its night time terror bombing campaign against British cities. His thoughts were increasingly centred on the potential threats in the Balkans and more importantly from Russia.

Even so, from a practical viewpoint, the autumn was certainly not the time to begin an invasion of Russia, as history had clearly demonstrated to Napoleon over a century earlier. Any invasion to the east would have to wait until the beginning of the following summer, a period that would also allow the *Luftwaffe* some time to recover from the damage and losses it had suffered at the hands of the RAF.

According to the records of the Quartermaster General of the *Luftwaffe*, from the beginning of May when the *blitzkrieg* started in Europe until the end of June, the *Luftwaffe* had lost 28% of its aircraft strength. When the Battle of Britain started in early July, it was still almost 900 aircraft short of its pre-*blitzkrieg* level, despite replacements. By the end of September, *Luftwaffe* losses had brought their aircraft strength down to 63% of the level of three months before, a statistic that shows how much it needed to re-equip before embarking on any large-scale operations either in the east or the west.

It was not until June 1941, when the invasion of Russia had begun, that the *Luftwaffe* regained operational strength equivalent to the levels of May 1940 when the offensive started against the Low Countries and France.

The fierce fighting over the south of Britain during the long summer of 1940 had also cost the *Luftwaffe* dearly in terms of experienced pilots and leaders. Despite the emergence of determined and skilled pilots as the war progressed beyond 1940, the *Luftwaffe* never really recovered from the crew losses that summer. Both sides in the conflict over southern Britain in 1940 had cause to mourn the loss of many skilled and irreplaceable pilots. For the Germans, the Battle of Britain had denuded them of many of the veteran pilots that had learnt their trade during the Spanish Civil War and the European campaigns culminating in the fall of France.

These could only be made up by intakes of inexperienced newcomers whose training, as in the RAF during 1940, had been seriously curtailed out of expediency. Parallel to the experience of the RAF over the summer of 1940, the life expectancy of many of these newcomers during the intensive combat sorties over southern England tended to be painfully short. The strain on experienced pilots on both sides increased daily as they were obliged to fly more sorties, as well as train the newcomers.

In the *Luftwaffe*, operationally-ready crew levels (those considered by *OKL* to be fit, trained and equipped for action) had fallen dramatically. For Bf 109 pilots, this had fallen from 869 pilots on the 1st of August 1940 to 673 pilots by the 1st of November 1940, underlining the heavy losses suffered during the summer assault on Britain. Bomber crews and those flying the twin engine Bf 110s, showed similar startling falls over this period, particularly in the case of the latter which had been heavily hit.

German aircraft production was also failing to keep pace with the losses of the increasingly critical single engine fighters. During the peak of the fighting from July to September 1940, the various plants producing the Bf 109 delivered some 700 aircraft. Over the same period, the German records show that a total of 703 aircraft were classed as damaged or destroyed, with 518 complete write-offs. This speaks volumes for the *Luftwaffe's* fitness to maintain the intensity of combat sorties that had been seen over August and September. By the autumn of 1940, it was clear that in order to continue to mount daylight bombing raids against southern Britain it was the single engine fighters that were critical. Here, aircraft losses were increasing and replacements were barely able to compensate for the sustained level of attrition.

RAF personnel sort through the wreckage of Luftwaffe aircraft shot down over Sussex at the Faygate depot, near Horsham, where most of this material from Sussex was gathered prior to being salvaged for production of new British aircraft. Recycling isn't as new as we thought! (MP)

The decline in the state of bomber crew readiness can be attributed to the level of physical casualties they had suffered and the effect these casualties had on the surviving squadron colleagues. While the British pilots may have had less success than they would have wanted in bringing down the bombers attacking Britain, the psychological impact of their attacks on the bombers' crews was significant.

In all three of the German medium bombers in the *Luftwaffe* arsenal, the *Heinkel* He 111, the *Dornier* Do 17 and the *Junkers* Ju 88, the crew was housed within the nose sections of these aircraft. All three, particularly the *Heinkel* which was perhaps the most widely used in the earlier part of the German assault, afforded little protection to attack from the frontal quarter. Their plexiglass nose sections offered little shelter from frontal attack, even though armour plating may have offered some from the rear.

With various British squadrons adopting the tactic of trying to break up approaching German formations by means of squadron strength head-on attacks, the level of casualties among the bomber crews was high, even if the bombers managed to regain their French bases. This had an understandable negative effect of the morale of the bomber crews.

One well-known British Squadron Leader was not shy to admit that he was more interested in causing casualties among the German bomber crews, rather than necessarily shooting down the aircraft. His logic was that badly-damaged bombers limping home with most of their crew either dead or badly wounded would have a sanguine effect on the willingness of the crews to press home future attacks on British targets, an obvious benefit. This was to some extent at odds with the comments of most fighter pilots, who traditionally viewed themselves fighting inanimate machines, rather than human beings of whatever political colouring. However, it explains in part the serious decline in bomber crew readiness over this period as the psychological stress of long daylight combat missions over Britain increased.

Starting from October 1940, the changing nature of the offensive raids by the *Luftwaffe* on Britain reflected these factors. No longer were huge formations of German bombers placed at risk of wholesale attack from RAF Fighter Command, which had demonstrated very clearly in September that it was far from the spent force that the Germans had hoped. From this point onwards, the *Luftwaffe's* medium bombers only crossed Britain's coastline during daylight in small groups with even larger fighter escorts. The daylight raids in October continued to focus mainly on London and the south, although other targets in the southwest and the Midlands were also attacked.

As summer finished and the days of autumn passed, modified Bf 109s, the *Jagdbombers* or "*Jabos*" (fighter-bombers) of the fighter units still on the Channel Front, began to account for the bulk of daylight bombing missions over southern England. While these could more easily penetrate to targets around London due to their higher speed and manoeuvrability compared to the *Heinkel*, *Dornier* and *Junkers* bombers, their limited bomb capacity - usually one 250 kg or four 50 kg bombs - and rudimentary bomb aiming ability, meant that these raids could only be of nuisance, rather than strategic value. Later in 1942 and 1943, different German *Jabo* tactics exposed the south of England in particular to an altogether more effective and frightening series of attacks.

A factory-fresh Messerschmitt Bf 109 E-4/B loaded with a 250 kg bomb on its centreline bomb rack.

The daytime *Jabo* missions that started on a more widespread basis as early as September 1940 initially caused no small amount of confusion among many British sector controllers in the south. German formations that did not contain a high ratio of bombers were still allowed to penetrate the southeast with limited response. When these early *Jabo* missions were undertaken, with the incoming aircraft normally at high altitude, it was embarrassing to find some targets were being bombed when no bombers had been detected in the attacking formations. These high flying formations of *Jabos*, accompanied by further fighter escorts, were difficult to counter without standing patrols or early, potentially-wasteful scrambles before their intended targets became clear.

While some of the *Jabos* operated by these units had force-landed in Britain in the early part of September, there seems to have been little recognition by RAF Intelligence of how the bomb racks fitted on such casualties altered the operational flexibility of the Bf 109. Needless to say, with daylight sorties by medium bomber formations all but ceasing from the beginning of October, this became unmistakeable.

Encouraged by the success of the first major Bf 109 *Jabo* sortie on the 20th of September, Goering instructed all of his *Jagdwaffe* units to modify one *Staffel* in each *Gruppe* to provide a fighter-bomber capability. During the weeks that followed, the required modifications were made, creating a force of some 200-250 Bf 109 *Jabos*.

While there were some notable dissenters who saw this as an unwelcome limitation to the normal fighter's role, the majority of the *Jagdwaffe* pilots employed in this way made the best of a difficult job.

The Bf 109 was always a difficult aircraft to manoeuvre while on the ground, above all during both take-off and landing. Carrying a bomb load during take-off was particularly dangerous and only experienced pilots were generally assigned to the *Jabo* role. Because of this, most *Jabostaffeln* were assigned to airfields which had concrete runways, rather than the converted farmland that they had used for the conventional fighters.

The *Jabo* raids in the autumn of 1940 remained of little strategic importance, but they had an unsettling effect generally on the south coast's population. As the war progressed beyond 1940, surprise raids by pairs of *Jabos* became a worryingly unpredictable occurrence for the south's coastal towns. These later raids frequently approached at high speed, wave-hopping below radar coverage. With many pilots anxious to drop their bomb load as soon as possible in order to regain the more agile performance values of the Bf 109 as a fighter, the British coast was an all-too tempting target. This would slacken off later in 1941, but resumed with a vengeance in the early summer of 1942 until finally petering out in the summer of 1943.

Over the last quarter of 1940, the main bombing offensive switched to night raids, where the medium bombers would wait till dusk before venturing into British airspace. Throughout the night and into the early morning, German bombers ranged over much of London, the south and the midlands, operating single aircraft or small group attacks in relays during most nights. British night fighting capability remained ineffective throughout the Battle of Britain, despite some well-publicised exceptions which were used to their maximum propaganda value in order to disguise the limited number of victories that were possible after dark.

In reality, the German crews were much less vulnerable to fighter attack once night had fallen, their main concern being anti-aircraft fire, barrage balloons, mechanical problems, weather and navigation.

Looking at the casualty reports for October 1940, it's clear that one factor became increasingly influential - the deteriorating weather. As October progressed, the problems faced by crews on both sides operating in increasingly poor visibility, fog, wind and rain, were reflected in aircraft that simply got lost, or ran out of fuel searching for home base. Neither side was equipped with the sort of modern day navigation aids that can offset these dangers today. Frequently, even in daylight, fighter interceptions became impossible in adverse weather conditions, and losses on both sides fell significantly from their summer peaks.

The effects of the seasonally declining temperatures were increasingly felt by the pilots. Some, scrambled from dew-laden airfields, found that their wet boots became frozen to the rudder pedals as they reached high altitude in their unheated cockpits. Frozen condensation on the inside of cockpits and windscreens caused many to go for novel counter measures, with rubbing a cut potato over the inside surface a favoured measure to minimise this. Condensation trails formed at much lower heights than during the summer and pilots frequently returned from sorties with cold-numbed hands and feet making it difficult to climb from their cockpits.

Local casualties 1st – 30th October

14.   Spitfire of 602 Squadron crash-landed on 7th October near Lullington

Daytime attacks on London continued, with both large and small groups of *Luftwaffe* aircraft crossing the Channel to venture towards London. Sometimes these attacks were made up of 120 or more aircraft, with three-quarters of these being fighters, escorting a small number of bombers. Frequently the groups were much smaller.

The 7th of October was a day of fair visibility and moderate cloud, with occasional showers. Late in the afternoon, Spitfires from 602 Squadron (call sign "Villa") had been scrambled to intercept a bomber formation that was detected heading for the Portland area. They were unsuccessful in intercepting this enemy group, but were asked by their controller to investigate a suspected target over the Brighton area. Pilot Officer Donald Jack as "Blue One" and Sergeant Basil Whall as "Blue Two", were detailed to investigate the contact.

"Ginger" Whall (DFM) had joined the Royal Air Force Volunteer Reserve (RAFVR) in 1936 and started his flying career at the beginning of the war with 605 Squadron. From April 1940, he had been transferred to 263 Squadron, where he had flown Gloster Gladiator biplane fighters against the Germans in the Norwegian campaign. After the withdrawal from Norway, he converted to Spitfires and was posted to 602 Squadron where he later earned his DFM. On the 14th of August, 602 Squadron was moved from Drem in Scotland into No. 11 Group and their home base became Westhampnett, Tangmere's satellite airfield, now Goodwood.

Local Home Guard soldiers pose for the camera in front of the Stuka dive-bomber forced to land at Littlehampton by "Ginger" Whall on 18 August 1940. The aircraft was part of II Gruppe StG 77 and landed with one crew dead while the other was taken prisoner. (MP)

Sergeant Whall was at the centre of the hectic air battles of *Adlerangriff*. He brought down a *Junkers* Ju 87 dive-bomber which force-landed on Ham Manor Golf Course near Rustington in the early afternoon of 18th of August. Shortly afterwards, he was himself obliged to force-land over Elmer Sands, near Middleton-on-sea. His Spitfire had sustained damage by return fire from a second dive-bomber that he had shot down in flames over the Channel. He was dazed but unhurt, and was helped from his written-off Spitfire by 23-year-old Lance Bombardier John Smith. From his vantage point at a searchlight site east of Middleton-on-sea, Smith had seen the aircraft struggling towards the coast and had rushed to help as it came to a stop in the shallows.

A week later, Whall shot down a *Heinkel* He 111 bomber that had been attacking Portsmouth Docks, with the German aircraft force-landing on East Wittering Beach. In early September, after bringing down a *Dornier* Do 17, he was wounded in the neck during an engagement with Bf 109s over Mayfield, but he succeeded in force-landing his badly-damaged Spitfire in a field near Arundel.

On the 7th of October, the suspected bomber over Brighton turned out to be another *Dornier* Do 17, momentarily spotted at about 1745 hours flitting from one cloud formation to another. With the German pilot unaware of the two Spitfires of Blue Section slightly above him, first Donald Jack then "Ginger" Whall attacked. Jack's burst of fire hit the starboard wing root and engine, while his colleague raked the centre section and cabin area. After briefly straightening out after the attack with no return fire coming from the German bomber, the *Dornier* crashed into the Channel with all crew on board.

"Ginger" Whall lies in Amersham Cemetery alongside the grave of his mother.

Instead of flying his normal Spitfire during this sortie, "Ginger" Whall had been flying the aircraft of one of his Squadron colleagues, "B" Flight's Commander, Flight Lieutenant Findlay Boyd. After the attack on the German bomber, the two Spitfires formed up for their return to Westhampnett, but "Blue Two" peeled off shortly after and started losing height without any warning. Donald Jack followed the aircraft down, screaming for his wingman to get out. There was an ominous silence from the Spitfire that was by then rapidly losing height.

"Ginger" Whall was clearly unable to exert full control over his aircraft, and he attempted a force-landing at Court Farm on the east side of the Cuckmere River, near Lullington. Sadly, whatever control he had must have been lost and he spun in during his approach to land, the aircraft exploding on impact.

Despite being rushed to Princess Alice Hospital in Eastbourne, he died on arrival. Basil "Ginger" Whall is now buried in the peaceful cemetery at Amersham in Buckinghamshire. He lies alongside his mother who sadly lost other sons during World War Two, like many of her generation.

With no obvious explanation for what happened, pilot blackout and even sabotage were suspected in a local wartime incident that remains a tragic mystery.

15. <u>Spitfire of 222 Squadron crash-landed on 27th October in Hailsham</u>

In typical autumn weather, mostly cloudy with some brighter spells during the early morning, German daylight raids on the 27th of October reflected the pattern of the last few days. Small groups of bombers crossed the coast in the southeast with their fighter escorts throughout the day, intent on attacking London and other targets in southern England. Four major raids were recorded, usually about 60 aircraft including 12-15 of bombers with the remainder fighters escorts.

222 Squadron, operating Spitfires from Hornchurch, was among the units sent to attack the *Luftwaffe* formations late that day. As the autumn light faded, one of the squadron's pilots experienced similar fuel problems to those that many German Bf 109 pilots suffered in the heat of action.

P/O Eric Edsall had joined 222 Squadron after recovering from injuries sustained during the bombing of Hornchurch at the end of August, when he was operating from that airfield with 54 Squadron.

F/O Alan Deere's Spitfire, blown onto its back by bomb blast during a raid on 54 Squadron's Hornchurch base on 31 August 1940. Eric Edsall's Spitfire was taking off at the same time and had its wing blown off.

While he and other squadron colleagues were attempting to take off during a bombing raid, his aircraft had been blown sideways, spinning around and landing upright. Despite a dislocated hip, he managed to get out of the aircraft and crawled to another Spitfire also badly damaged by the falling bombs. This was F/O Alan Deere's machine, which had been blown upside down by the blast, trapping Deere in the cockpit, hanging in his harness. Edsall eventually managed to wrench off the cockpit door and helped Deere to escape. A third Spitfire, piloted by Sergeant Davies, was also damaged trying to take off.

By late October, Edsall had shot down four German aircraft, but during dog-fighting with Bf 109s over the south coast on the 27th of October, his Spitfire ran out of fuel and he was forced to look for a likely site to bring his aircraft down safely. Whether due to the failing light or simple error, in selecting the fields of Pattenden's Farm on Battle Road in Hailsham, he made the mistake at 1800 hours of flying through some power cables as he came down and crashed heavily. P/O Edsall was seriously injured in the crash and was rushed to Hellingly Hospital for treatment, leaving his aircraft a complete write-off.

Eric Edsall was later awarded the DFC on the 16th of January 1942, but was killed at the age of 24 in a Japanese attack on Ceylon on the 12th of April 1942.

Aftermath

Aftermath

So as the days of autumn 1940 grew shorter, the list of casualties on both sides did the same. Daylight sorties by the *Luftwaffe* continued in a desultory fashion as much as the deteriorating weather allowed, dominated by the mostly high altitude *Jabo* attacks that caused little strategic damage. Combat losses fell away as the weather conditions hindered effective daylight raids, at the same time frustrating interceptions by British pilots.

In Sussex, the casualties during the last two months of 1940 were mainly British, with very few German aircraft falling within the county's boundaries. Most of those that did were bombers, unlucky victims of anti-aircraft fire or the fledgling British night fighter force. British casualties over this period covered the full range of aircraft types operated by the RAF - bombers, fighters and training aircraft - many of which suffering from the uncompromising winter weather, as well as enemy action and mechanical failure.

The German night bombing offensive continued throughout the winter, with terror raids on London, Coventry and other parts of the country. These caused enormous damage and horrendous civilian casualties, and ultimately led to RAF Bomber Command, together later with the USAF, conducting a bomber campaign against German industry and cities.

For Fighter Command, the last days of October 1940 marked the end of the hectic defence of southern England that had started nearly four months earlier. Churchill did not stint in his praise for the bravery and sacrifice of the British pilots, and rightly so. At a time when Britain and the Commonwealth still stood alone against the forces of Germany and its allies, to some degree recovered from the defeats in Europe during the early summer, something positive was needed to strengthen public morale. Using his well-honed skills as a public orator and political manipulator, Churchill focussed justifiable attention on the victories achieved by RAF Fighter Command and the effect these had in frustrating any German invasion plans.

The autumn also brought some less savoury developments at Fighter Command. The simmering antagonism between the Air Ministry and the Commander-in-Chief of Fighter Command came to a head with the ignominious transfer of both Dowding and Park to other duties. Looking back, it's possible that the Air Ministry hierarchy felt the need to remove them from centre stage. Dowding and Park had arguably become too successful in the defence of Britain's southern airspace. They had achieved this by adopting strategies that were the contrary to the policies promoted by Trenchard, seen as the "Father of the RAF", who had overseen its creation at the end of the First World War and guided its development thereafter.

Like many after World War One, Trenchard saw a strong bomber force as the logical way to defend Britain from attack. Maxims along the lines of "the bomber will always get through" and "the best means of defence is offence" were central to this belief. Most expenditure and research for the RAF was therefore concentrated on developing the bomber force, fighter development staying in the background until the early 1930s, when the spectre of German rearmament raised serious questions over this emphasis.

By the autumn of 1940 however, it was clear that it had been largely through Dowding's stubborn development of a strong and modern fighter force, supported by a unique early warning and control system, that the German airborne assault had been rendered ineffective. Without fighters, what would have defended the British bomber bases from attack, so how could more bombers improve Britain's level of defence? The Air Ministry accordingly pushed Dowding and Park as far away from the limelight as possible, in doing so minimising the risk that its mistaken emphasis on bombers during the inter-war years would be seen for what it was. The stress on bomber development had arguably put Britain's defence at risk.

Despite gentlemanly pressure from the King and Winston Churchill to honour Dowding's contribution, the Air Ministry was determined that both he and Park should be shuffled aside at the earliest opportunity. In 1941, the Air Ministry published a booklet focussing on Fighter Command's efforts during the Battle of Britain. It made no mention whatsoever of Dowding's role. This caused

Churchill, when he was made aware of the omission, to order the booklet to be reprinted, making Dowding's contribution clear and honouring his efforts

The faster and more complicated Junkers Ju 88 progressively replaced both the Heinkel He 111 and Dornier Do 17 bombers on the few daylight missions that continued as the autumn passed. The slower bombers were dedicated mainly to the night bombing campaign.

With neither Dowding nor Park having the time or inclination to cater to the niceties of the political manoeuvring required in many parts of the military and civil service hierarchy at the time, it came as no surprise to some that they became victims of jealousy and intrigue within the Air Ministry. On the 25th of November, Air Vice-Marshall William Sholto Douglas, Deputy Chief of the Air Staff at the Air Ministry, was appointed to take over Dowding's position as Commander-in-Chief of Fighter Command, while his predecessor was dispatched on a mission to the U.S. It was a public relations exercise for which Dowding's character was ill-suited, so it was a failure.

Some three weeks later, Keith Park, the brilliant controller of No. 11 Group's defence of London and the southeast during the hectic summer months, was transferred to No. 23 Group Flying Training Command. He arrived in December 1940 to find that they were working at only two-thirds of capacity, following what were effectively peacetime practices. Had either Dowding or Park suspected this was the case during the peak of the summer conflict, when pilot losses became such a controversial issue, it would undoubtedly have become a subject for further dispute with the Air Ministry. Before he was transferred in January 1942 to take over responsibility for the air defence of the Nile Delta, he made sure this bottleneck received the attention it needed to correct this potentially disastrous failing.

Park was later to take over the air defence of Malta in July 1942, where he further distinguished himself, again facing his old adversary, the former commander of *Luftflotte 2*, "Smiling Albert" Kesserling, against whom he had so successfully conducted the defence of southern Britain over the summer of 1940.

Aftermath

As AOC No. 11 Group, Park was replaced by his nemesis from No. 12 Group, the ambitious Trafford Leigh-Mallory, with whom he had so often clashed during the summer months. Then Park's complaints frequently centred on the speed with which Leigh-Mallory's squadrons responded to his request for them to cover his airfields while his own squadrons were sent to meet the incoming German bomber fleets.

Leigh-Mallory and the outspoken Douglas Bader, one of the squadron commanders in his group, both favoured combining several squadrons together in what was termed a "Big Wing". The aim of this was to fight force with force and to intercept the *Luftwaffe* raids with 30-50 aircraft, and so destroy more aircraft than was possible with smaller groups.

Another problem with the Big Wing concept was that the larger the opposing formations became, the more confused were the interceptions and the numbers of aircraft destroyed became disproportionately low, relative to the numbers involved. Because of this, subsequent analysis of the claims made by the "Big Wing" formations has showed that it encouraged over-claiming. In a large dogfight where many aircraft are involved, the need to avoid collision with either side was a natural

barrier to identifying the final outcome of snap bursts fired at targets that fleetingly appeared in front of your guns. The "Big Wings" were not unique in this, but their numbers merely made it easier to fall into that trap.

Air Vice-Marshall Sir Keith Park, who played such an important role in the defence of southern England during the Battle of Britain. (Sir Keith Park Memorial Campaign)

While the sight of such a formation undoubtedly had a salutary effect on the German pilots who were continually being told that the RAF were down to its last few fighters, one of its major drawbacks was that it took a comparatively long time for all the aircraft to rendezvous together. No. 11 Group's airfields were occasionally left undefended as No. 12 Group marshalled several squadrons together. Bader maintained that it didn't matter whether you hit the bomber formations before they had dropped their bombs, or while they were returning to their French bases, as long as they were hit hard.

Park however could not afford to leave his airfields open to bomb damage that would progressively make his airfields inoperable. His own tactics in No. 11 Group were primarily aimed at breaking up the German bomber formations before they were able to reach their targets, essential in August and early September in order to limit the damage to the airfields in the south. In a pattern that would immortalise the concept of "The Few", hugely outnumbered as they attacked German formations that normally numbered in excess of 500 aircraft, he dispatched successive squadrons, sometimes singly but frequently in pairs, against the approaching *Luftwaffe* formations. This meant that there were frequently up to two dozen British fighters intercepting a mass of German aircraft. The British fighters would then usually split up, with some aircraft taking on the escorts, while the others hit the more important bombers.

Once the German attacks were focussing on targets in and around London, by scrambling squadrons as soon as practical after the German aircraft crossed the English coastline, he gave them the best chance of reaching sufficient height to break the incoming attacks, as well as allowing a sensible rotation of squadrons to land, rearm and refuel. Sometimes, the British fighters were held back from attack until the German formation had reached the London outskirts, by which time the Bf 109 pilots were focussed on their fuel warning lights, in order to ensure they had sufficient fuel to get back to France.

When the battle was at its peak and it was essential to commit all of his squadrons to intercept the German raiders, Park needed aircraft from both Nos. 10 and 12 Groups to protect his vulnerable but crucial airfields. He had no problems with No. 10 Group, but the same was sadly not the case with No. 12 Group. Dowding was later to acknowledge that he should have exerted more control over what effectively became petty antagonism between the two sector controllers.

As 1941 loomed and daylight defence of the southeast became a less pressing requirement than it had been over the summer of 1940, No. 11 Group squadrons under Leigh-Mallory began to assume virtually the identical roles that the *Jagdwaffe* had between July and October 1940. Bomber Command's offensive against occupied Europe gathered pace and, for daylight bombing operations, it was mainly No. 11 Group's squadrons that acted as escorts.

The same fuel problems and the barrier of the Channel that had hampered the *Luftwaffe* over the summer of 1940 now presented similar obstacles to the British pilots' safe return to England. No. 11 Group's new AOC also favoured squadrons being involved in offensive sweeps to draw up the *Jagdwaffe* units bases in France, with the aim of inflicting as many casualties as possible, as well as attacking targets of opportunity. In the mirror image of the *freie Jagd* sorties by the *Jagdwaffe* during the summer of 1940, it was rare that the German fighters took the bait.

Most of the German fighter units that had been operating from the Pas de Calais area and parts of northwest France had been withdrawn from the Channel Front for rest and refitting in preparation for the offensives against the Balkans and Russia. The majority of these had been exhausted from their continuous operations since May 1940 and the debilitating losses suffered during the Battle of Britain. From 1941onwards, only two fighter wings remained to counter the threats from Britain. JG 2 continued to operate from its base in Beaumont-le-Roger in Normandy, and JG 26 spread their different *Gruppen* at various locations around Calais. At the beginning of September 1940, there had been five times as many Bf 109 units, as well as four units equipped with the Bf 110.

Through 1941 and beyond, the majority of aircraft casualties in the Eastbourne area continued to be British aircraft of one sort or another, gradually supplemented by U.S. aircraft once the USA entered the war from the end of 1941. Most of these Allied aircraft were returning from missions over Europe, frequently damaged and low on fuel.

Sussex began to suffer different problems, with Eastbourne achieving the unenviable reputation of being the most raided town on the south coast. German raids on the area were on a smaller scale than had been seen over southern England during the summer of 1940, but the damage and fatalities that these caused were nonetheless equally painful. Hit and run sorties were more frequent than the sort of massed formation attacks of 1940. German raiders, usually the *Jabo* fighter-bombers that began to operate on daylight sorties from the autumn of 1940, were occasionally brought down in the local area.

As 1941 began, Hitler demanded that the *Luftwaffe* should conduct concerted terror raids against London and the southeast. His aim was damaging not only military targets and British industry, but also continuing to undermine the morale of the civilian population. This was partly to reduce the ability of Britain to send military support for Russia, against which he launched his offensive in June 1941. It was also in retaliation for the British bombing offensive against Germany and occupied Europe.

Frequently, these later raiders operated in pairs, approaching the coast at sea level under the range of radar coverage and then attacking towns along the south coast, where railway sidings and gas works were favoured targets. Sometimes, larger *Jabo* formations would be sent to attack targets further inland, escorted by their *Jagdwaffe* colleagues. The Sussex coast became a regular focus for these *Jabo* raids from the spring of 1941 until they ceased in the early summer of 1943.

April 1942 heralded a further change in the German bombing strategy against Britain. With the tempo of British bombing raids against both Germany and occupied Europe gathering pace, Hitler authorised a more indiscriminate level of attacks against Britain. A teletype message from his Headquarters to the *Luftwaffe* Operations Staff dated the 14th of April 1942 signalled this more ominous period for Britain's south coast.

> *The Fuehrer has ordered that the air war against England is to be given a more aggressive stamp. Accordingly, when targets are selected, preference is to be given to those where attacks are likely to have the greatest possible effect on civilian life. Besides ports and industry, terror attacks of a retaliatory nature are to be carried out against towns other than London. Mine-laying is to be scaled down in favour of these raids.*

Many of the modern buildings we see around Eastbourne today were built on the sites of bomb damage from this period, often curious, soul-less structures that should find no favour with planning authorities of today. The east wing of the Cavendish Hotel, Metropole Court (formerly the site of the Metropole Hotel), the Borough Treasurer's Building in Grove Road and the blocks of flats along much of Bourne Street are but a few examples.

The afternoon of 4 May 1942 saw nine Messerschmitt Bf 109s from 10/JG 2 scattering bombs and gunfire throughout Eastbourne, causing widespread damage including the east wing of the Cavendish Hotel, on the seafront opposite the band stand. (TRB)

It was difficult to counter these surprise raids. Unlike the *Jabo* sorties of autumn 1940 where the fighter-bombers tended to attack from high altitude, they now approached the coast virtually at wave-top height, giving little chance for British squadrons to position themselves to attack before the *Jabos* were already on their way back to France.

Nevertheless, some of these were damaged, and others crashed in the sea off Eastbourne and Beachy Head. A few suffered more visible fates. Until late 1942, most of these were brought down by light anti-aircraft fire, either from the 40 mm Bofors sites or light machine guns such as the Bren or Lewis.

Fighter Command later realised that the only aerial defence against these raids was to mount standing patrols at sensitive target areas, something that was not put into effect until November 1942. Thereafter, it was not uncommon for some of the raiders to be caught by British fighters.

At midday on the 20th of May 1942, *Unteroffizier* Oswald Fischer of the 10th (*Jabo*) *Staffel* of JG 26 took off on his 31st *Jabo* mission, leading a *rotte* of two *Messerschmitt* Bf 109 F-4 fighter-bombers, their target shipping in the Newhaven-Brighton sector. After flying in low over the coast, the two aircraft approached Newhaven from inland and dropped their bombs on a corvette in the harbour roads. Heavy fire from the vessel bracketed both aircraft and Fischer's "White 11" (*W. Nr.* 7232) was hit, damaging the all-important coolant system.

With Crapham Barn and the mist-shrouded cliffs between Belle Tout lighthouse and Birling Gap in the background, Oswald Fischer's Messerschmitt Bf 109 F-4 fighter-bomber is examined by RAF personnel near Halfway Cottages. (TRB)

Fischer's Messerschmitt Bf 109 F-4 being test flown after an engine replacement in 1943, sporting British camouflage colours but still retaining its former aircraft and unit identifications marks, as well as the yellow tactical markings on the lower engine cowling.

With his engine overheating and faltering, and too low to contemplate crossing the Channel, Fischer ordered his wingman to return to France. Preferring a force-landing on solid ground to the potentially fatal delights of the Channel, he turned back for the English coast near Beachy Head. He made a successful, wheels-up landing on Crapham Hill, near Halfway Cottages and close to the

Aftermath

B2103 leading to Beachy Head, not far from Crapham Barn. Coincidentally, this was less than a mile from where Horst Perez had landed the East Dean Bf 109 that started my researches.

After trying unsuccessfully to blow up his downed aircraft, Oswald Fischer was captured and joined many of his earlier colleagues as a POW. His aircraft was later repaired and flown by No. 1426 (Enemy Aircraft Flight) of the RAF, whose role was to fly captured enemy aircraft types in order to familiarise Allied personnel with their recognition features and performance. Shown here under evaluation by RAF personnel after an engine replacement and test flights on 24 October 1943, Fischer's Messerschmitt Bf 109 F-4 was given the British registration NN644, but retained the unit insignia of 10/JG 26 despite repainting in British markings.

Three months later, on the 26th of August 1942, the pilot of a *Focke-Wulf* Fw 190 A-3 fighter-bomber, also from 10th (*Jabo*) *Staffel* of JG 26, was less fortunate when his aircraft was brought down over Lottbridge Drove. One of a pair of *Jabos* on a hit and run raid on Eastbourne's electricity generating plant at Roselands, off St. Phillips Avenue, "Black 13" (*W. Nr.* 2080) came under fire from a Bren gun operated by Canadian troops stationed on the roof of nearby Caffyn's garage, then at the junction of Seaside and Lottbridge Drove.

The fin and aft fuselage of Werner Kassa's Focke-Wulf Fw 190 "Black 13", also from 10th Staffel JG 26, buried on the edge of one of the drainage ditches along the path of today's Lottbridge Drove after being shot down on 26 August 1942. (CGC)

After releasing its bomb load, the *Focke-Wulf* was hit while it banked as the pilot attempted to escape back over the Channel, crashing inverted in one of the many drainage ditches in the area, slightly to the west of the current Lottbridge Drove. The pilot, *Oberfeldwebel* Werner Kassa, was killed in the crash and Private E.G. Johnstone of the Canadian Seaforth Highlanders was given credit for bringing the aircraft down. Werner Kassa's wingman, *Obergefreiter* Richard Wittmann, fared a little better, although his aircraft was also damaged by ground fire as he made his escape. He returned to his base outside St. Omer without seeing his *Rottenfuehrer* crash.

Between the crash-landing of Oswald Fischer's *Messerschmitt* Bf 109 in May and Werner Kassa's ill-fated mission on the 26th of August 1942, the 10th *Staffel* JG 26 had finally been re-equipped with the new radial-engine *Focke-Wulf* Fw 190.

Aftermath

This new aircraft had caused major problems for RAF Fighter Command from its first operational introduction, since it was faster and more manoeuvrable than the Spitfire Mk V that was the predominant variant then in service. The Fw 190 had the advantage over the *Messerschmitt* Bf 109 F in having an air-cooled radial engine behind an armour-plated cowling ring, making it less vulnerable to ground fire. It was also more manoeuvrable at the lower altitudes necessary for most *Jabo* sorties compared to its predecessor. JG 2, then the only other *Jagdwaffe* unit on the Channel Front, had followed a similar timetable for re-equipment with the Fw 190, designed by Kurt Tank, who went on after the war to help the Argentinian Air Force make the transition into the world of modern aviation.

Eastbourne's electricity plant was devastated by one of the two bombs dropped during this raid. Its former site now houses the town amenity and recycling depot at the junction of St. Phillip's Avenue and Churchdale Road. The other bomb destroyed several houses in nearby Marlow Avenue, leaving several civilians dead and injured.

Just before a later mission, a 10th Staffel JG 26 Jabo pilot completes his engine checks at the unit's base at Wizernes, near Calais. The Focke-Wulf Fw 190 was ideally suited to the dangerous ground attack roles that the Jabo pilots adopted over 1942 and 1943. (CGC)

This type of raid became a regular feature of the town's daily life as the war continued, slackening during the winter months, but always remaining a threat until they ceased in the middle of 1943. Between the early summer of 1942 and the middle of 1943, Eastbourne became the focus of at least 13 of these so-called "tip and run" raids. Like many south coast towns with various large private schools and numerous hotels, these buildings in Eastbourne had been taken over by the military for one purpose or another. Arguably, this gave these raids some military value, but from the early summer of 1942, civilians were just as likely to be targeted as military, port or industrial areas.

107

Aftermath

Before these *Jabo* attacks petered out in the summer of 1943, Eastbourne and its surrounding towns and villages had frequently witnessed at close hand the physical and psychological effect of the surprise raids. Polegate and Hailsham shared in the terror that these low level bombing sorties brought between the end of 1942 and the beginning of 1943.

By mid 1943, pressure to increase the numbers of fighters available to oppose mostly American daylight bomber raids on Germany and the rest of occupied Europe forced *Luftwaffe* High Command to disband most of the *Jabo* units. These were incorporated into regular fighter groups or into fighter-bomber units defending southern Europe and Italy. While the need to defend Germany against the daylight bomber attacks was real enough, this move demonstrated yet again that German Intelligence was unaware of how damaging these "tip and run" raids had really proved to be.

Already suffering the effects of more than a dozen *Jabo* raids between the spring of 1942 and the summer of 1943, Eastbourne had the dubious honour of being subjected to the last two mass *Jabo* attacks during daylight on England. From the early part of 1943, these sorties had started to cross the English coast not in pairs, but in squadron strength or occasionally larger groups, frequently with separate fighter escort. By this time, it became common for targets to be attacked by two dozen or more fighter-bombers at a time.

Understandably blurred, this unique photograph was taken Lt. "Poldi" Wenger, a Jabo pilot with IV/SKG 10, as he swept fast and low towards the gas works after crossing the Downs above Meads on 4ᵗʰ June 1943. (CGC)

On the 4ᵗʰ of June 1943, 18 *Focke-Wulf* Fw 190 fighter-bombers streamed low over the coast between Birling Gap and Beachy Head, observed fleetingly by the military units stationed at both locations. The German aircraft were all from IV.*Gruppe / Schnellkampfgeschwader* 10 (SKG 10), formed during the early part of 1943 by amalgamating the *Jabo* units from both JG 2 and JG 26. They crossed the ridge of the Downs above Meads and dropped down into the coastal bowl of the town, breaking into smaller groups heading for different parts of the town. They attacked the usual targets around the railway station in the centre of town and the gas works near Lottbridge Drove, as well as buildings in the Meads and seafront areas.

Among the pilots flying this mission was *Leutnant* Leopold "Poldi" Wenger, who had been flying *Jabo* missions against southern Britain with the 10th *Staffel* of JG 2 since the end of May 1942. On many of the sorties that he flew, Wenger was in the habit of taking photographs as he attacked the various mission targets. He was finally killed in action in April 1945, but his amazing collection of photographs was made available by his surviving brother to the well-known aerial historian, Chris Goss. You get a vivid impression of how low these *Jabo* pilots flew, probably no higher than 300 – 400 feet, certainly low enough to get the unwelcome attention of the Civil Aviation Authority today!

Flak positions around the town damaged a number of the *Jabos*, and although two Spitfires from 41 Squadron based at Friston did manage to intercept the German formation as it returned to France, they had little success. Only one of the raiders was brought down, hit by a light AA fire from a site that had recently been taken over by Scots troops. After his *Focke-Wulf* was hit, *Oberleutnant* Kurt Hevler attempted to make a force-landing, but died when his aircraft overturned as it struck a drainage ditch near the Star Inn at Normans Bay.

The memorial stone for Oberleutnant Kurt Hevler at the German War Graves Commission cemetery at Cannock Chase, one of hundreds maintained by the Commission's staff.

Aftermath

Finally, on the 6th of June 1943, more than two-dozen *Focke-Wulf* Fw 190s approached Eastbourne at wave top height after midday, this time crossing the coast from the southeast over the Crumbles and dropping a series of 500 kg bombs over the town, causing considerable damage. On this occasion, the raiders were from II.*Gruppe* / SKG 10. Seven civilians and a number of military policemen were killed during this last raid, and there was extensive damage right across the town.

The escaping aircraft strafed the Royal Observer Corps outpost at Beachy Head, their wooden hut taking numerous hits from the *Jabos'* cannons and machine guns. At East Dean, local Air Warden P.J. Budd made a note in his daily report that some of the escaping aircraft had also strafed several buildings, particularly in Friston. Damage was caused to various buildings and numerous unexploded cannon shells were later found.

Despite damage from ground fire around Eastbourne, all of the aircraft managed to return to base with one exception. *Leutnant* Dominikus Miller of 7th *Staffel* / SKG 10 was intercepted over the Channel and shot down by two pilots in Spitfires from 91 Squadron, P/O Dennis Davy and Sergeant John Patterson.

Underlining the Luftwaffe High Command's curious lack of strategic awareness, the only *Jabo* group remaining on the Channel Front to attack England from mid 1943 was dedicated to night sorties. *OKL* was either unaware of the impact surprise daylight raids were having on the civilian and military population particularly around the south coast, or their importance was dismissed. Night attacks by single aircraft at random locations over southern Britain did nothing like the damage that the daylight sorties had done, and so they remained ineffective.

The *Jabo* offensive of 1942 and 1943, directed along the length of England's south coast and parts of the east coast, came to a halt. In contrast to the haphazard use of *Jabos* during the closing stages of the Battle of Britain, the later "tip and run" campaign had proved both damaging to Britain's war economy and demoralising to the civilian population. The earlier raids were frequently conducted by large formations, attacking from high altitude, readily picked up by Britain's radar defences and mostly focussed on the principal target of the time - London. The 1942/43 *Jabo* campaign was completely different and wholly effective in terms of the damage achieved versus the level of pilot loss.

These later raids, mostly at sea level, focussed mainly on strategic targets, railway facilities, gasworks and shipping, many of which were regularly damaged or destroyed. However, by this stage of the war, earlier restrictions on attacking civilian targets had also long ago been lifted, and the *Jabo* pilots and their occasional escorts were encouraged to pursue "terror" attacks on targets of opportunity - buildings, the general population and livestock. The effect of this on the conduct of life in the south was dramatic, and a collective sigh of relief was all but audible when the summer of 1943 passed with no resumption of the daylight *Jabo* campaign. By the time Germany's doodlebugs and V-2s started to land randomly all over the south in 1944, public anxiety again became a feature of daily life.

On the night of the 8th/9th November 1943, Shinewater Marsh, between Hampden Park and Stone Cross, saw another German raider crash. A *Messerschmitt* Me 410 was shot down over the town by a De Havilland Mosquito night fighter from 85 Squadron, flown by Squadron Leader Bill Maguire with his radar operator Flying officer W. D. Jones. By this stage of the war, both the RAF and the *Luftwaffe* had been able to produce radar units that were small enough to mount in this type of aircraft, allowing night-time interception to become a more regular occurrence than it had been in 1940. The RAF had Mosquitos and Bristol Beaufighters for this purpose, while the *Luftwaffe* was able to give the *Messerschmitt* Bf 110 an altogether more productive second lease of life as a radar-equipped night fighter.

The Me 410 bomber exploded violently, leaving the marshy ground with a large crater containing the disintegrated remnants of the airframe and the remains of the two crew members. They were finally identified in the 1970s through some serial numbers on a scrap of metal as *Major*

Aftermath

Wilhelm Schmitter and *Unteroffizier* Felix Hainzinger. Schmitter had been a highly decorated officer holding the Knights Cross with Oak Leaves, the envied target of many *Luftwaffe* pilots like Helmut Wick who died chasing medals and fame off the Needles during November 1940 (see local casualty number one).

A Messerschmitt Me 410, the final piston-engine fighter-bomber replacement for the Bf 110 which suffered so badly during the Battle of Britain. The Me 410 was based on the Me 210 which had design faults that prevented it from entering Luftwaffe service in significant numbers.

The airstrip at Gayles Farm, near Friston, was gradually brought into operation as a forward fighter base for operations across the Channel. During the Battle of Britain, this small airstrip on the downland between the Cuckmere and Friston had only been used as an emergency landing field. It did not act as an operational base until May 1941, when Westland Lysanders from 225 Squadron started operations, using Friston as a satellite airfield to their home base at Shoreham.

The airfield was briefly used as a decoy fighter base between May and June 1942, complete with dummy aircraft, some of which were probably made in Hailsham by Green Brothers in Western Road. It appears that these didn't fool the *Luftwaffe* though, since there are no records of the airstrip being attacked during that summer. It didn't come to full operational status until later in June 1942, when a succession of squadrons used it as a satellite base. Some of the sorties flown from Friston were in support of the disastrous Dieppe raid of August 1942. Other missions from this small airfield were as bomber escorts over Europe or as interceptors against the "tip and run" attacks that caused no small amount of havoc around the south coast.

By 1944, Belgian pilot Freddie Moureau was regularly flying Spitfires from the Friston airstrip with 349 Squadron. He survived potentially fatal crashes during his time operating from the airstrip. In January 1944, he was made a force-landing at Herstmonceux, northeast of Eastbourne. At the end of April that year, Jesse Taylor recalls witnessing another close call while he and some friends were working in the fields between the airstrip and the Seven Sisters cliffs. Pilot Officer Freddie Moureau encountered serious engine problems that forced him to crash-land his Spitfire in nearby Gate Field, suffering serious injury in the process. A touching story follows on from this potentially fatal adventure.

While Freddie was recovering from his injuries in Princess Alice Hospital in Eastbourne, Stan Hobden, one of the local farmers who pulled the pilot from his Spitfire's wreckage, suggested to his daughter, Hazel, that it might be a friendly gesture to go and visit the Belgian pilot in hospital.

Aftermath

She duly followed her father's suggestion, resulting in her later marrying Freddie at East Dean in 1945. After the war, they moved to Belgium where Freddie continued flying for the state airline, Sabena. After 24 years in Belgium, the couple moved back to the village and now live in the Friston, less than two miles from the site of the old Friston airfield.

On the night of the 14th of March 1944, a *Dornier* Do 217 bomber was shot down not far from the Friston airstrip. All the crew on board were killed when it struck the downland slopes overlooking the Cuckmere estuary with the loss of all on board.

The remainder of the war saw many more aircraft casualties along the coastal strip around Eastbourne but, increasingly, these became allied aircraft returning from missions over Europe.

Sited at the spot where the B-24 Liberator "Ruth-less", from the 506th Squadron, 44th Bombardment Group, 8th USAAF, crashed on 2 February 1944, the local community has erected a memorial stone commemorating the crew's loss overlooking the town. A memorial service is regularly held in their honour.

Overlooking Eastbourne, near Foxhole Brow just off the South Downs Way, lies a plaque, commemorating the loss of ten American airmen who died on the 2nd of February 1944. Their B-24 Liberator bomber ("Ruth-less") had been hit by enemy flak while on a daylight mission over France, bombing the area around the huge underground V-1 (doodlebug) assembly factory at Watten in the Pas de Calais. With one engine out of action and a second barely operating, the bomber tried an approach to Friston airfield near Gayles Farm. It was turned away because of congestion at this small airstrip and the B-24 chose to follow the coast eastwards round Beachy Head towards Eastbourne, always struggling for height.

As it crossed the Eastbourne coast, the crew must have realised that they had only a narrow chance of clearing the ridge of the South Downs, shrouded in mist and low cloud. Nevertheless, as the aircraft passed over Ocklynge and Old Town with their engines screaming at full power, the crew waved to the townspeople below. With barely more than half of their normal output, the engines could not overcome gravity. "Ruth-less" slammed into the hillside a few feet below the ridge of the Downs, and all on board were either killed outright or died shortly afterwards.

As the allied bombing offensive built up from 1942 onwards, Friston airfield was frequently used as an emergency field for force-landings by American bombers returning, like "Ruth-less", damaged or low on fuel from daylight missions over Europe. Another B-24, "Heaven can wait", operating out of Shipdam, Norfolk, the same home-base as "Ruth-less", tried to use the field as an emergency airstrip on the 12th of March 1944 after a mission over France. Sadly the aircraft crashed and was completely burned out.

The now disused airstrip was more recently the site of a fictional fighter base for the filming of "Piece of Cake", a tale of fighter pilots during the early part of World War Two. I remember the filming going on and getting close enough during the last days of filming to watch the replica Spitfires and airfield buildings being destroyed by explosive charges to simulate the German bombings called for by the storyline. This was quite spectacular at the time.

From my youth, I can still recall the wartime airfield's concrete nissen huts mouldering in the windswept hawthorn and may bushes lining the border of the field where the A259 runs westwards. These, like many of the surface structures erected during the war, have disappeared over time.

Concrete foundation blocks for the transmitting and receiving aerials of Pevensey Chain Home RDF station are visible reminders today of the site's role during the Battle of Britain. Today this is part of Pylons Farm, on the marshy fields between Pevensey and Hurstmonceux, with the old Observatory telescope domes on the horizon.

Aftermath

Not so, however, for some of the more substantial buildings that needed masses of concrete or large underground structures. When my family moved to East Dean in the mid 1950s, Beachy Head was dominated, not just by the holiday image of the red and white lighthouse on the rocks below, then still operational, but also by the radar station with its constantly rotating aerial.

This was not the radar station that operated on this site during the Battle of Britain, but a post-war installation, commissioned in 1954 and finally demolished in 1963. Nevertheless, it's still possible today to locate the sealed-off entrances to various underground chambers that would have protected vital personnel and equipment from attack. In the 1950s and 1960s, the perceived threat would have been from potential Soviet incursions, typical of the Cold War years that followed World War Two and the Korean War.

On Pevensey Levels, the remains of the Pevensey Chain Home RDF Station that was one of the four targets of the surprise raid by *Erprobungsgruppe 210* on the 12th of August 1940 are still there to be seen.

After decommissioning in 1958, the lower section of the operations building was converted into the farmhouse now called Pylons Farm. In the fields alongside the farm stand the massive foundations for the two sets of masts that transmitted and received the signals of approaching aircraft, surrounded by the usual farm debris of discarded machinery and grazing animals. Additional forlorn concrete structures over these fields conceal the entrances to unidentified underground chambers over this marshy landscape that was the location during the summer of 1940 of more aircraft casualties than I'd imagined when I started this project.

Not surprisingly, the passage of almost seven decades has left few other physical reminders of the hectic days during the summer of 1940 and the aircraft that were forced down around the Eastbourne area at that time. The countryside remains much as it was, albeit more densely-populated and covered with housing developments than it was then.

The fields around Mays Farm, near Selmeston, where two German fighters came to earth during that summer, understandably show no sign of the experience, while around Pevensey and Langney, a similar story holds true. "Hill Brow" on Gaudick Road in Meads remains much as it was on the 16th of August 1940 before the body of the unlucky Ernst Hollekamp crashed into it, the gable end now invisibly repaired.

Just southeast of the Sovereign Harbour entrance channel, low tide today reveals the three rusting boilers of the S.S. Barnhill, whose bombing on 20 March 1940 initiated Eastbourne's long and painful exposure to aerial attacks from the Luftwaffe in 1940.

Aftermath

Low tide at the Crumbles Marina reveals the still slowly eroding boilers of the S.S. Barnhill, the unexpected provider of extra food rations for local villagers after it broke up off the coast in early 1940.

In Hailsham, Percy Burton's heroic endeavours on the 27th of September are marked by the small pathway named in his honour off Station Road, as well as by the moot witness of the sad splintered oak tree into which his disintegrating Hurricane crashed.

Closer to home, 800 meters from my house, an overgrown crater on the upper slope of Crapham Down marks virtually the spot where the Bf 109 of Horst Perez came to earth, the machine that started this meander through the wartime experiences of the area. I thought the crater may have been the result of some stray bomb exploding later in the war rather than anything related to that incident, but Jesse Taylor assures me the crater had been there long before the war, perhaps the site of earlier flint excavations.

The *Messerschmitt* that Horst Perez managed to land on the ridge of the downs above East Dean now sits renovated on display at Duxford, a uniquely-visible and stark reminder of those dark days in 1940, when young pilots on both sides lost their lives, faithful to their countries' leaders and contemporary patriotic fervour.

The graves of the airmen, both Allied and German, that perished of course also remain visible to those that seek them out. The Allied pilots that served in the Battle of Britain are all recorded on the numerous memorials that have been erected in recognition of their sacrifices. Their graves tend to be scattered throughout the country, some close to where they fell and some returned to their community churchyards.

With the evening sunshine filtering through the birch and pines at Cannock Chase in Staffordshire, the German War Graves Commission cemetery reflects the typical scenery of some parts of Germany. It's a fitting and peaceful setting to reflect on the waste of life suffered by both sides over the pivotal summer months of 1940.

Aftermath

Most of the German airmen who died over southern Britain were initially buried close to where they fell, where some still remain. A few, like Horst Liensberger, were returned after the war to their home towns, to be re-interred. The majority however lie at Cannock Chase, Staffordshire, where the German War Graves Commission maintains a cemetery for German war dead from both World Wars.

With patriotism today a more complicated concept for many to understand outside of international sporting contests, when you're wandering around the frequently musty and sterile displays of twisted and unrecognisable aircraft wreckage at different museums around the country, it's easy to appreciate how difficult it must be for children and young people today to understand the passions, courage and fears that must have driven the young pilots that flew in that summer of 1940. I hope perhaps some of what is written here may stimulate at least some of the pride and admiration that I have developed for all of the men that demonstrated both their courage and national identity during those brief hectic and dangerous months.

Bibliography

Bishop, Patrick, *Fighter Boys*, Harper Perennial 2004

Brooks, Robin J., *Sussex Airfields of the Second World War*, Countryside Books 1993

Bungay, Stephen, *The Most Dangerous Enemy*, Aurum Press 2000

Burgess, Pat & Saunders, Andy, *Battle over Sussex 1940, Blitz over Sussex 1941-42, Bombers over Sussex 1943-45,* Middleton Press 1990/2004

Butler, Phil, *War Prizes*, Midland Counties Publications 1994

Caldwell, Donald, *The JG 26 War Diary Vol. One 1939-1942*, Grub Street 1996

Collier, Richard, *Eagle Day, The Battle of Britain*, J. M. Dent & Sons Ltd., 1966-1980

Deighton, Len, *Fighter*, Jonathan Cape Ltd. 1977, *Battle of Britain*, Jonathan Cape Ltd. 1980

Goss, Christopher H., *Brothers in Arms, The Luftwaffe Fighters' Battle of Britain, Luftwaffe Fighter-Bombers over Britain,* Crecy Books Ltd., 1994, 2000 and 2003

Green, William, *Famous Fighters of the Second World War*, Macdonald & Co. 1957/1960

Holmes, Tony, *Hurricane Aces 1939-40*, Osprey Publishing 1998

Huggett, Colin J., *A Place in Time,* 2002, *Waters Edge,* 2003

Humphrey, George, *Wartime Eastbourne the story of the most raided town in the South-East*, Beckett Features 1989

Johnson, J.E. (Johnnie) & Lucas, P.B. (Laddie), *Glorious Summer*, Stanley Paul & Co. Ltd. 1990

Levine, Joshua, *Forgotten Voices of the Blitz and the Battle for Britain*, Ebury Press 2006

Lucas, Paul, *Camouflage & Markings No. 2 The Battle for Britain - RAF May to December 1940*, Guideline Publications 2000

Michulec, Robert, *Messerschmitt Me 109 pt. 1*, A-J Press 2001

Mombeek, Eric (Smith & Creek), *Jagdwaffe Attack in the West May 1940*, Classic Publications 2000. Mombeek, Eric (Wadmann & Creek/Wadmann & Pegg), *Jagdwaffe Battle of Britain Phase One July-August, Phase Two August-September, Phase Three August-September, Phase Four September-October 1940* Classic Publications 2001/2002

Murray, Williamson, *The Luftwaffe Strategy for Defeat 1933-1945*, Eagle Editions 2003

The National Archives, Kew, Surrey, various historical documents including pilot combat and POW interrogation reports and squadron operation records

Neil, Wing Commander Tom J., *Gun Button to "Fire"*, William Kimber & Co. Ltd. 1987

Bibliography

Price, Dr. Alfred, *Battle of Britain: The Hardest Day 18 August 1940*, Macdonald and Jane's Publishers Ltd., 1979, *Spitfire Mark I/II Aces 1939-41*, Osprey Publishing 1996/2005

Ramsey, William G. *The Battle of Britain Then and Now*, Battle of Britain Prints International Ltd. 1985

Ries, Jr. Karl, *Markings & Camouflage Systems of Luftwaffe Aircraft in WW2*, Verlag Dieter Hoffmann 1966

Ritger, Lynn, *The Messerschmitt Bf 109 Part 1 Prototype to E Variants*, SAM Publications 2005

Robinson, Derek, *Invasion 1940*, Constable & Robinson Ltd., 2005

Rowland, David, *Spitfires over Sussex*, Finsbury Publishing 2000

Scott, Peter, *The Messerschmitt Bf 109E on the Western front 1940*, Guideline Publications

Scutts, Jerry, *Combat Legend Messerschmitt Bf 109*, Airlife Publishing Ltd. 2002

Vasco, John J., *Zerstoerer Volume One*, Ian Allen Publishing Ltd. 2005, *Bombsights Over England*, JAC Publications 1990,

Vasco, John J & Cornwell, Peter D., *Zerstoerer*, JAC Publications 1995

Von Eimannsberger, Ludwig, *Zerstoerer Gruppe*, Schiffer Publishing Ltd., 1998

Wadman, David & Pegg, Martin, *Jagdwaffe Holding the West 1941-1943*, Classic Publications 2003

Watson, Kevin, *Ruth-less and far from home*, Kevin Watson 2000

Weal, John, *Messerschmitt Bf 110 Zerstoerer Aces of World War 2*, Osprey Publishing 1999

Glossary of terms and abbreviations

Abteilung 5
This was the *Luftwaffe's* intelligence department.

Abwehrkreis
Formations of *Messerschmitt* Bf 110 heavy fighters and fighter-bombers would frequently adopt this formation over southern England in which the individual aircraft of the formation flew in a circle with each aircraft covering the aircraft in front. Often called a defensive circle, it was frequently used for this purpose later in the summer when the heavy aircraft were under attack from more nimble, single engine fighters. It was also used in the early days of the battle, since the spectacle of a *staffel* or *gruppe* of these aircraft circling overhead was very visible. It was intended as an attempt to lure British fighters into the air in an effort to neutralise RAF fighter command's strength.

Adlerangriff (Eagle Attack)
This was the code name for the *Luftwaffe's* air assault against Britain in 1940.

Adlertag (Eagle Day)
This was the code name for the first day of the *Luftwaffe's* air assault against Britain in 1940.

AOC
Air Officer Commanding was the title for the officer in charge of individual RAF Fighter Command Group areas.

Bf
For the sake of simplicity, the two fighters (109 and 110) manufactured and supplied to the *Luftwaffe* during the Battle of Britain by *Messerschmitt* are shown with their model numbers prefixed by Bf, short for *Bayerische Flugzeugwerke*. There was a complicated chain of model ownership between *Messerchmitt Flugzeugbau*, *Bayerische Flugzeugwerke* and *Messerschmitt AG*, Willy Messerschmitt's own company. It's common for all *Messerschmitt* aircraft of this period to be referred to with the Me prefix before the model number, but it seems more likely that both the 109 and the 110 models should have the Bf prefix and all later models the Me prefix, e.g. M*e* 210/410/163/262, etc.

Bordfunker
This was the *Luftwaffe* term describing the role of radio operator/gunner, particularly commonplace for the second crew member in the *Messerschmitt* Bf 110 heavy fighters and fighter-bombers of the period.

British Expeditionary Force (BEF)
British Army and RAF units assisting the defence of Belgium, Holland and France.

Chain Home
This was the term describing the series of radar sites located around the coast of Britain, with the only gaps being in the northwest of Scotland, the Bristol Channel and a portion of the Welsh coast. There were 21 sites (CH) designed to identify formations at high altitude at the start of the Battle of Britain, and a further 30 sites (CHL) designed to identify formations at low level or shipping.

Der schwarze Donnerstag
This was the German term for Thursday the 15th of August 1940, when the *Luftwaffe* suffered its heaviest losses during the summer of 1940.

Erprobungsgruppe
Operational test wing dedicated to trials of new aircraft or tactics in front line service. *Erprobungsgruppe 210* was the most prominent unit that used this title during the summer of 1940.

Experten
The *Luftwaffe* gave this title to pilots who had five confirmed aerial victories to their name. It's similar to the "ace" term used by the Allies.

Feldwebel (Fw)
This was broadly equivalent to Flight Sergeant in the RAF.

Freie Jagd

This term applied to the offensive sorties conducted by German fighter units, frequently with no specific target laid down, but generally aimed at enticing British fighters up from their airfields so they could be engaged and destroyed.

Generalfeldmarschall

In recognition of their contribution to the victories that Germany had won since the autumn of 1939, Hitler promoted both Kesserling and Sperrle from *General der Flieger* to the rank of *Generalfeldmarschall*. This was a rank broadly equivalent to Marshall of the Royal Air Force.

Geschwader

This was broadly equivalent in aircraft numbers to a Group in the RAF. There would normally be a Headquarters' Flight of 3-4 aircraft as the *Geschwaderstab*, with at least three *Gruppen*, each with their own Headquarters' flight of 3-4 aircraft together with three *Staffeln* of 13-15 aircraft. At full operational strength, the *Geschwader* would have some 150 aircraft.

Geschwaderkommodore

This was the commander of a Group within the *Luftwaffe*, applicable for both fighters and bombers, broadly equivalent to a Group Captain in the RAF.

Gruppe(n)

Roughly equivalent in aircraft numbers to a Wing in the RAF, there were normally three *Gruppen* to each *Geschwader*, each with a complement of 40 - 45 aircraft, although this was frequently smaller or larger, according to operational requirements and losses. Each *Gruppe* was subdivided into three *Staffeln*, as well as a small headquarters' (*Stab*) flight. The *Gruppe* number was always shown as a Roman numeral.

Gruppenkommandeur

This was the rank given to the leader of a *Gruppe*, which was broadly equivalent to the rank of Wing Commander in the RAF in terms

of the numbers of aircraft controlled. He would normally hold the rank of *Major* or *Oberstleutnant*.

Hardest Day

The 18th of August 1940 saw both sides of the conflict suffering heavy losses and became known by this term.

Hauptmann

This was broadly equivalent to a Flight Lieutenant in the RAF.

Idiotenreihen

This was the term used by German fighter pilots viewing from above a British fighter squadron in its regulation V or line astern close formation. It translates as "the row of idiots".

Jagdbomber (Jabo)

This term referred to any of the *Luftwaffe* fighters that operated as fighter-bombers during the Battle of Britain, irrespective of whether these were *Messerschmitt* Bf 109s or Bf 110s.

Jagdfliegerfuehrer (Jafu)

This post was created in both *Luftflotten* 2 and 3 as the assault began against Britain towards the end of July 1940. Theo Oesterkamp became *Jafu 2*, based in the Calais area and further west, the role of *Jafu 3* fell to Werner Junck. As the need to minimise the fuel problems of the Bf 109 increased, the latter's importance declined with most of these aircraft falling under the control of *Jafu 2*.

Jagdgeschwader (JG)

Luftwaffe fighter group of single engine aircraft.

Jagdwaffe

His was the generic term for the fighter component of the *Luftwaffe*.

Kampfgeschwader (KG)

Luftwaffe bomber group.

Glossary of terms and abbreviations

Kampfggruppe
Luftwaffe bomber wing.

Kanalkampf
The initial phase of the Battle of Britain where the main German air attacks were directed against Channel convoys and coastal facilities on the south coast.

Kanalkampffuehrer (Kanakafu)
Head of Channel Operations at the start of the *Luftwaffe* offensive against England.

Kanalkrankheit
Common term used by German aircrew to describe their anxiety of flying over the English Channel. It became normal for many German airmen to need a desperate visit to the squadron latrines after mission briefings for this reason.

Lehrgeschwader (LG)
These were operational training groups within the *Luftwaffe*, deployed in 1940 to develop various tactical techniques. LG 2 operated two *Gruppen* equipped with Bf 109s, the first, *Jagd* (fighter), unit operating normally as conventional fighters and the second, *Schlacht* (ground attack), as *Jabos*.

Leutnant (Lt)
This was broadly equivalent to Pilot Officer in the RAF.

Luftflotten 2,3 and 5
The *Luftwaffe* was divided into independent (*Luftflotten*) Air Fleets on a geographical basis, each operating its own fleet of aircraft covering the full range of operations within the *Luftwaffe*, i.e. fighters, bombers, transports, reconnaissance or rescue aircraft. *Luftflotte 2* was based in Brussels during the summer of 1940 and had the main task of attacking southeast England and the London area. *Luftflotte 3* was based in Paris with their main target focus being the south and southwest of England and the industrial Midlands. *Luftflotte 5* was based in Stavanger

in Norway and apart from a brief foray against the northeast of England in mid August 1940, limited their operational focus to defending the coast from Germany to Norway, as well as conducting shipping strikes in the North Sea.

Luftwaffe
The German Air Force.

Mae-West
The nickname given to the RAF standard issue inflatable vest used by aircrew in the event of landing in water. The name referred to the obvious attributes of the Hollywood film actress of the same name.

Major
This was broadly equivalent to a Squadron Leader in the RAF.

Obergefreiter (Obgefr)
This was broadly equivalent to a Leading Aircraftsman in the RAF.

Oberkommando des Heeres (OKH)
German Army High Command.

Oberkommado der Luftwaffe (OKL)
Luftwaffe High Command.

Oberkommando der Wehrmacht (OKW)
Overall High Command for the German armed forces.

Oberleutnant (Oblt)
This was broadly equivalent to the rank of Flying Officer in the RAF.

Oberst
This was broadly equivalent to the RAF rank of Group Captain.

Reichsmarschall
On the 19th of July 1940, Hitler appointed Hermann Goering as his second in command, creating for him the new rank of Marshall of the German Reich and marking the occasion by handing Goering an elaborately crafted baton, signifying his elevated position of

power. It speaks volumes for the closeness between Goering and Hitler at that time, in that Hitler felt it necessary to make a special gesture to his trusted ally from the start of the rise of National Socialism in Germany since the early 1930s. This was to some degree the result of the promotion of both Kesselring and Sperrle to the rank of *Generalfeldmarschall*, in recognition of their contribution to the victories that had been achieved since September 1939. Goering had previously been the sole officer of this rank in the Armed Forces.

Rotte(n)
The basic formation for German fighter pilots, comprising two aircraft with the leader protected by his wingman throughout a sortie.

Schlageter
JG 26 adopted the unit name of *Schlageter* in honour of Albert Leo Schlageter who was executed in 1923 after a resistance mission against French occupying troops in Germany after World War One. With the rise of National Socialism in Germany in 1933, he became a hero of the Nazi party. JG 26's unit emblem adopted in his honour showed a black gothic script letter "S" on a white shield.

Schwarm
Two pairs of German fighters operating in a loose, finger-four formation.

Seeloewe (Sea Lion)
Code name for the German invasion of southern Britain.

Seenotflug Kommando
These were the *Luftwaffe's* air-sea rescue units using mainly *Heinkel* He 59 seaplanes, white-painted biplanes showing the red cross.

Stab
The headquarters' flight of either a *Geschwader* or a *Gruppe*, usually made up of 3 - 4 aircraft operated by the Commander of the unit, the Adjutant, the Technical Officer and occasionally another staff rank officer.

Staffel(n)
This was roughly equivalent in aircraft numbers to a squadron in the RAF. The *staffel* number was always shown as an Arabic number.

Staffelkapitan
This was the rank given to the leader of a *staffel*, which was broadly equivalent to the rank of Squadron Leader in the RAF in terms of the numbers of aircraft controlled in action. In the Battle of Britain, the role of the *Staffelkapitan* usually depended on the experience and skill of the individual, rather than rank. In the early part of the conflict, his aircraft would be identified with the number "1", as well as carrying a small triangular pennant attached to the radio antenna aft of the cockpit.

Stuka
This was the commonly-used name for the *Junkers* Ju 87 dive-bomber, actually an abbreviation of *Sturzkampflugzeug*, or dive-bomber. It gained a terrifying reputation among both civilians and the military on the ground from the Spanish Civil War until the summer of 1940. Used as aerial artillery in the support of an advancing ground offensive with limited opposing aircraft, it was an effective tool in the German arsenal. It was more vulnerable and generally less effective against Britain, which represented a fixed defensive position with a well-organised control network and modern, agile fighters.

Unteroffizier (Uffz)
This was broadly equivalent to Corporal in the RAF.

Wehrmacht
The German Armed Forces.

Werke Nummer (W. Nr.)
German aircraft manufacturers assigned production numbers to completed aircraft for reference and spare parts reasons.

Zerstoerer

This was the name by which the *Messerschmitt* Bf 110 twin engine heavy fighter was generally known. Goering saw the units equipped with this aircraft as his elite units, able to provide fighter escort to bomber sorties deep into enemy territory. The aircraft had many positive features, but in close combat with agile single engine fighters it was revealed to be too cumbersome to turn and unable to accelerate quickly enough to survive. Some versions equipped for dive-bombing during the Battle of Britain were also delivered from the factories with the name *Jaguar* emblazoned on the fuselage nose.

Zerstoerergeschwader (ZG)

This was a fighter wing equipped with twin engine (Bf 110) fighters.